The Equine Athlete
How to develop your horse's athletic potential

Also from BSP Professional Books

Horse and Stable Management
Jeremy Houghton Brown and Vincent Powell-Smith
0 632 02141 1

Equine Injury and Therapy
Mary Bromiley
0 632 02277 9

Getting Horses Fit
Sarah Pilliner
0 632 02307 4

Keeping Horses
How to Save Time and Money — A Guide for the Working Horse Owner
Susan McBane
0 632 02363 5

Pasture Management for Horses and Ponies
Gillian McCarthy
0 632 02286 8

How to Keep Your Horse Healthy
Colin Vogel
0 632 02056 3

Practical Stud Management
John Rose and Sarah Pilliner
0 632 02031 8

Horse Business Management
Jeremy Houghton Brown and Vincent Powell-Smith
0 632 02184 5

The Competition Horse
Breeding, Production and Management
Susan McBane with Gillian McCarthy
0 632 02327 9

The Equine Athlete

How to develop
your horse's athletic potential

Jo Hodges
and
Sarah Pilliner

OXFORD
BSP PROFESSIONAL BOOKS
LONDON EDINBURGH BOSTON
MELBOURNE PARIS BERLIN VIENNA

BSP Professional Books
A division of Blackwell Scientific
    Publications Ltd
Editorial offices:
Osney Mead, Oxford OX2 0EL
25 John Street, London WC1N 2BL
23 Ainslie Place, Edinburgh EH3 6AJ
3 Cambridge Center, Cambridge,
    MA 02142, USA
54 University Street, Carlton,
    Victoria 3053, Australia

First published 1991

Set by Best-set Typesetter Ltd., Hong Kong
Printed and bound in Great Britain by
Hartnolls, Bodmin, Cornwall.

DISTRIBUTORS

Marston Book Services Ltd
PO Box 87
Oxford OX2 0DT
(*Orders:* Tel: 0865 791155
         Fax: 0865 791927
         Telex: 837515)

USA
    Blackwell Scientific Publications, Inc.
    3 Cambridge Center
    Cambridge, MA 02142
    (*Orders:* Tel: (800) 759-6102)

Canada
    Oxford University Press
    70 Wynford Drive
    Don Mills
    Ontario M3C 1J9
    (*Orders:* Tel: (416) 441-2941)

Australia
    Blackwell Scientific Publications
    (Australia) Pty Ltd
    54 University Street
    Carlton, Victoria 3053
    (*Orders:* Tel: (03) 347-0300)

British Library
Cataloguing in Publication Data
Hodges, Jo
    The equine athlete: how to develop your
    horse's athletic potential.
    1. Livestock. Horses. Training
    I. Title   II. Pilliner, Sarah
    636.1088

ISBN 0-632-02622-7

Contents

Acknowledgements

The authors would like to thank clients and colleagues, Marian for the typing, and especially George Hodges for all his help and support, without which this book would not have been written.

The exercises which appear in Chapter 12 are reproduced from *Goodbye Backache* by Dr David Imrie with Colleen Dimson. The authors have made every endeavour to trace the copyright holder for this material but have been unable to achieve this.

Introduction

This book is designed to help riders and trainers develop the full athletic potential of their horses so that they can perform better and their competitive careers can continue longer.

To help achieve its full potential, each individual horse must be looked at as a whole and then detailed analyses made of specific areas. The following chapters will show how each area can be assessed and monitored, and will also discuss methods and techniques that can be used to improve and help the individual horse.

No horse is perfect in body or temperament; assessment of the individual allows his best points to be developed and his weaker ones to be attended to, resulting in a horse that is less likely to 'go wrong'.

An essential part of looking after competition horses is the treatment of soundness problems. One of the aims of this book is to emphasise the importance of looking at the *causes* of the problems and how they affect the whole horse and its performance. Merely treating the signs may result in temporary relief but the problem may return, perhaps in a more intense form. As the demands of competition increase, it is inevitable that success will depend upon attention to the finest detail; some of these details include individual training programmes, developing the horse's physical and psychological capacity for his work, preventing and treating small injuries, helping him recover from fatigue, and making the most of rest periods so that the body can heal itself effectively.

The value of sports therapy for keeping the athlete in first class condition and for rehabilitation after injury is well recognised by human sports people and athletes. This book hopes to ensure that the equine athlete receives the same sort of treatment with the associated long-term benefits.

We can only give you our opinions based upon our experience and the research we have carried out. There are many roads to Rome, but we believe this to be the best.

1
The ideal equine athlete

One of the aims of this book is to show you how to collect information about your horse, and how to record the data for future use. This is the concept of profiling, which gives you a personal record of your horse that contains essential information about your horse and monitors his progress.

The idea is to train you to record as objectively as possible your observations of your horse. It is important that these are your observations, and yours alone, as it is your future observations which will be monitoring development. You will find that as you become more knowledgeable and more aware of your assessment abilities your confidence will grow.

Your concept of what your horse looks like will be governed by your attitude to the horse, previous experience of horses and your present knowledge. In the past you may have had a particular horse or pony which you thought was nearly perfect, so that all that breed, colour or type of horse creates a positive feeling. On the other hand, you may have the opposite experience with another breed or colour, so that similar types make you respond negatively. The horse will of course pick up these feelings from you and no doubt will conform to your expectations! You may have had ambitions for your horse which are beyond either his capabilities or his present development. This could be the cause of frustration and anxiety for you and also for your horse, which in the circumstances is probably being unfairly pressurised and therefore confused and may lose confidence in his master. This of course can have a cumulative effect, causing a breakdown of the relationship between horse and rider.

Before profiling and assessing our own horses we must forget our prejudices and instead have an ideal to work towards. We must therefore give some thought to what constitutes the ideal equine athlete.

The athletic horse conforms to certain criteria which are common to all horse activities, be it dressage or racing. If we close our eyes and think of our ideal, the picture would no doubt feature a superb animal bursting with pride, presence and good health, containing and confining his energy and waiting with eagerness for instructions from his rider or driver. He portrays confidence in his body and his ability, he is perfectly balanced, and he is beautifully proportioned and symmetrically developed. His action and carriage are smooth, graceful and harmonious. His performance ability is at the level you as a rider are happy with. What a paragon!

As we come back to earth and consider how many factors are involved in first finding and then producing a horse of such virtue, or just bringing out the full potential of our horses, we find that the list is indeed very long and the cost great. In reality things are not so clear cut and life is full of compromises. However, if, when buying a horse, we consider good conformation, equal proportions, good development and temperament, we will get the most from our limited budget. Defects in conformation may lessen the chances of a horse staying sound during his training, and incorrect development will produce physical stress that will then affect the temperament. A good temperament and attitude to work will make him a pleasure to own and manage.

Temperament

The horse's temperament and attitude must be considered in relation to your chosen sport and how it will stand up to the demands of the necessary level of training.

Many horses will perform in the company of others and hate doing things on their own. Some will get better with training; others never perform well. It can be surprising what a hunter can do out hunting or on the point-to-point course, but try and take him across country on his own and it may be a different picture! Others will perform better on their own and hate competing against others: some like showing off whereas others are ring shy.

A horse that can accept travelling, excitement, change of stable and crowds with a spark of interest and a sense of the importance of the occasion but with the laid-back attitude that accepts it all as a day's work will lose little weight and suffer from little nervous tension. Physical stress levels are high enough in competition work without adding temperament stress on top.

An important point to be considered when we are thinking about the temperament and the character of the horse is your own temperament. It is commonly thought that caring and riding a pony is good character development for children, because they have to put the pony's needs before their own and learn their own strengths and limitations and how to deal with frustration and to make the best of a situation. The more we know about our own strengths and weaknesses of character, the more we can develop the best parts and control the bits we do not like, and the better we can adapt to different types of horse. A certain type of horse can bring out the best in you and another can bring out the worst. Some trainers and riders know this. They know that they will not bring out the best in a particular type of horse, and will not even think of taking it on: a very sensible approach.

Think about what is important to you in a horse's temperament. We know from experience that some horses that are said to be 'nappy' can change if given to someone of a different temperament and with different attitudes. Everyone knows that a little loving care goes a long way, and some big commercial yards may not have the time to accommodate animals which need more time and human contact. In contrast the individual owner may enjoy the horse that needs extra attention, and will therefore be able to bring out the very best the horse has to offer.

A dog will show his love by showing affection, wagging his tail, and licking his owner. A horse cannot show affection in this way, but the more you give to your horse in care and thought the more the horse will give you in honest work or cooperation. Self-confidence, cooperation and willingness are vital considerations when judging a horse's temperament.

Conformation

What is conformation? A horse's conformation, what he looks like or the way he is put together, consists of two aspects:

(1) the skeleton;
(2) the muscle, fat and skin covering the skeleton.

Horses ideally should be skeletally correct with correctly developed muscles, adequate subcutaneous fat and a covering of supple healthy skin and hair. A horse that is skeletally incorrect can be disguised with well developed muscles and a thick layer of fat deceiving the eye. It is important to train the eye so that it is not fooled by superficial correctness because, as we have mentioned, conformational defects can affect the horse's soundness and usefulness. We need to be able to assess a horse's conformation, decide the areas that are not so good, and plan how to develop him to support these weaker areas.

Our assessment and opinion of a horse's conformation will also depend on which activity we wish the horse to follow. Each activity presents a different objective in terms of speed, strength, stamina and learned skills, each calling for certain conformation differences.

Many people would say that a proportioned horse of good conformation could be trained to perform successfully in any of the different disciplines provided his temperament and attitude fit the kind of work. There may be a great deal of truth in this, but there are some conformation proportions that are more important for some disciplines than for others.

The perfect equine athlete is just a concept: we do not know what the perfect shape is, or the perfect temperament, or the perfect way to develop them. Such things may not exist! All that can be done is to look at as many horses as possible that perform consistently and successfully at a high level and have a good attitude to their work, look for similarities in their conformation, and assume that these similarities contribute towards their athletic success.

However, a great deal of a horse's success depends on the expertise of the rider, trainer and stable manager and the time they are able to spend, regardless of his conformation. Remember that each rider and trainer will have different preferences and ways of training and riding, and will have formed their opinions from their experiences of many different horses. Our initial assessment of a horse's conformation will involve looking at how the horse is put together, and at his development, his proportions and of course the way he moves. The higher up the ladder you wish to go determines the degree of perfection you are looking for. Good skeletal conformation and good development do not necessarily give good performance, but successful function does usually depend on correct form and consequently good conformation and development make an excellent starting point.

Proportion and Development

Equal proportions and symmetrical development are very important in determining the way the horse will move and perform. In order for a horse to be naturally balanced, his centre of mass has to be correctly placed. If it is too far forwards he will be too heavy on his forehand, and if too far to the rear he will put strain on his lower back (Fig. 1.1). If unequally proportioned between front and hindquarters, he will not have either the freedom or the power necessary for stride length and impulsion. How his head is fitted to his neck and his neck position in relation to his shoulders will influence the type of work for which he is most suitable; a high degree of collection will favour one type of conformation whereas a racehorse will reach out and get a longer stride with a different conformation.

The long-distance horse has to carry the rider for long periods and move with a gait that gives endurance rather than power. His back must be the area of conformation strength as his legs and feet will take more strain if there are any problems in the back and the loins. He will need to be a smooth comfortable ride so the rider can remain as still as possible and avoid fatigue.

Good feet which are in proportion and in balance, with the correct

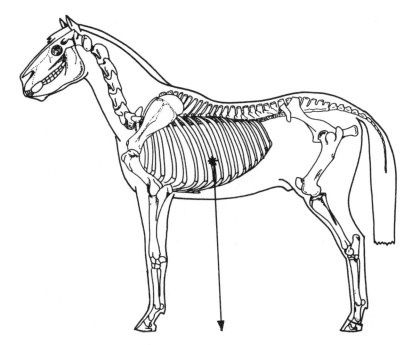

Fig. 1.1 Approximate location of centre of mass (*) in the standing horse.

degree of angulation of the whole foot continuing into the pasterns and the fetlocks, are extremely important. The limbs should as far as possible be in proportion and as free from blemish as possible, and the joints and the bones should give good alignment. The joints should be large and sufficiently angulated to accommodate the necessary muscle/tendon insertions without deviations between bones and joints, and give a good base for support.

The position and shape of the horse's pelvis in relation to the spine and the length of the rib cage and loins will determine how well he will withstand the stress and strain of work and of carrying a rider. The longer the horse is expected to carry the weight of the rider the more important these aspects become.

Ideal Conformation

Our ideal equine athlete should be alert and have presence and quality, and his head should be in proportion to the rest of his body with a bold eye and room at the jowl to allow for flexion. His head will be set on to his neck in such a way as to allow him to flex his neck and relax his jaw, giving a correct outline. His neck should be elegant, long and well set on to a sloping shoulder and well defined wither, which should

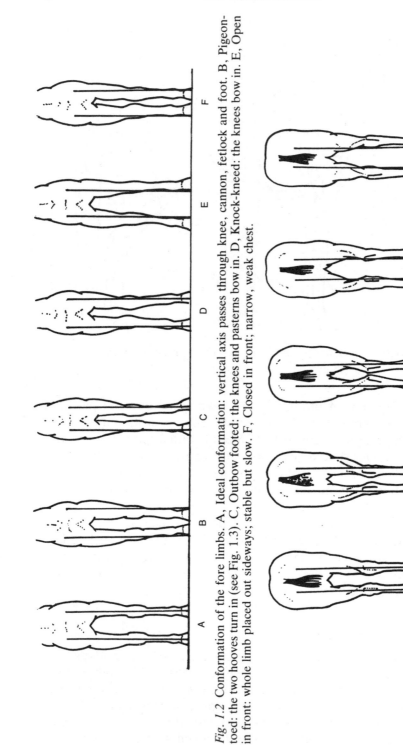

Fig. 1.2 Conformation of the fore limbs. A, Ideal conformation: vertical axis passes through knee, cannon, fetlock and foot. B, Pigeon-toed: the two hooves turn in (see Fig. 1.3). C, Outbow footed: the knees and pasterns bow in. D, Knock-kneed: the knees bow in. E, Open in front: whole limb placed out sideways; stable but slow. F, Closed in front; narrow, weak chest.

Fig. 1.4 Conformation of the hind limbs. G, Ideal conformation, vertical axis from point of buttock through hock, cannon, fetlock and foot. H, Closed behind; narrow and weak. I, Cow-hocked: hocks turn in; may lead to bone spavin in time. J, Too open behind; stable and powerful. K, Bowlegged: hocks turn out.

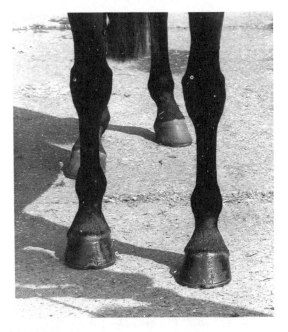

Fig. 1.3 Turned-in toes.

be higher than the croup. His chest should be neither too narrow nor too broad and have plenty of depth to allow room for his lungs and heart. The elbow should be free, the forearm long and strong and the cannon bone short with plenty of good, flat bone (Fig. 1.2).

The hooves should be a pair and symmetrical and open, and the angle through the hoof and pastern should not deviate and be about 45° in front and 50° behind. The back should be strong and of adequate length and in proportion to both forehand and hindquarters. The hindquarters are the powerhouse of the horse, and he should have plenty of length from the point of hip to the hock: in which case the hocks are described as 'well let down'. The hock joints should be well defined and turn neither in nor out. A vertical line from the point of buttock should coincide with the line from the point of hock down to the ground (Fig. 1.4). A horizontal line from the hocks to the knees should run almost parallel to the ground.

Conformation for Different Disciplines

Ideal conformation for the racehorse will vary depending on whether he is a sprinter or a stayer. Rather, his conformation dictates the type of race in which he is most likely to be successful.

A sprinter needs explosive power for a very short time, and is usually

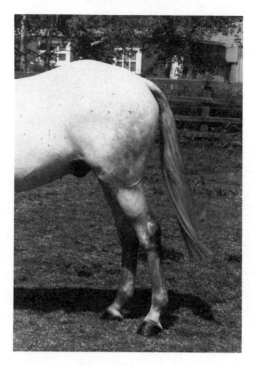

Fig. 1.5 Straight hocks. These may give speed but are not considered ideal.

smaller and very compact compared with the longer distance horse and the jumper, which need more stamina and are usually longer and more angular. As a sprinter will carry the jockey for only short periods, its greatest priorities are to gallop and stretch over very substantial fences.

The three-day-event horse has to be a jack of all trades and adept at very diverse activities and able to cope with the demands of the training. He must be able to work in a round outline and be supple and obedient to the slightest request of the rider. Further he must be able to gallop over steeplechase fences, show endurance during the roads and tracks phase, and jump huge fences across country. Finally, on the third day he has to jump a round of show jumps, which he knows are more easy to knock down, and still be obedient and athletic. Thus the three-day event is a supreme test of stamina and training.

Movement

As you watch the horse move, there should be no interference in the action of the limbs which could cause an injury or a fall. The path of the feet and the body of the horse should be as straight as possible, giving freedom and regularity to his movement. How the horse places his foot upon the ground and the balance of the weight on the foot are also important. The length of stride should be balanced between the fore and hind limbs, and the degree of flexion of the joints of the limbs should be the same; in other words the hocks should be flexed equally. The length of time the foot is on the ground has a lot of significance in the horse doing fast work: the longer the limb is on the ground the greater the compression to the internal tissue and the more stress the limbs receive. A picture of harmony and lightness is what you hope to see. Any compensation for incorrect development or discomfort will show in the horse's movement and carriage, causing bad posture which will affect his limbs and feet. Conversely, problems with his feet or limbs will affect his posture or outline.

Choosing the Equine Athlete

Buying horses is fraught with difficulty. Finding adequate funds appears to be the biggest problem but in reality this is just the beginning! In order to rationalise your selection, have a series of questions and a routine that you follow when looking at a horse. This prevents you from being carried away by the fact that you have just 'fallen in love' with this horse — not a good criterion for selection.

- Observe the horse's attitude and stance in the box: this will give clues to temperament, previous handling and minor aches and pains.
- Examine the legs for heat, swelling, thickening and bony lumps. Observe which leg or legs the horse rests and the way in which he rests it.
- Ask about the horse's feeding and fittening programme, and consider this with respect to the horse's condition. Feel his coat and skin for dehydration and lack of subcutaneous fat.
- Look for obvious conformation problems and stress problems related to work, e.g. windgalls, thoroughpins.
- Look for any deviation of alignment in the limb bones and signs of interference, e.g. scars from brushing.
- Pick up each foot and observe the shoeing for uneven wear, foot balance, evenly sized feet and the state of the fect.
- Check shoulders, back, neck and hindquarters for well and evenly developed muscles.
- Pick up all four feet and very quickly assess the degree of movement in the knees, hocks and fetlocks.
- Run your fingers firmly down his spine and note any reaction and any lumps that should not be there.
- Check the ears and eyes for normal reflexes.

- Age the horse and quickly assess the suitability of his mouth for carrying a bit.

Having assessed the horse in the stable and noted any potential problems, ask to see him outside to see if these problems are manifested in any peculiarities in his movement.

- Observe at walk: look for an active walk with a clear four-time beat, an even amount of overtracking from both sides and no stiffness as the horse leaves the box.
- Observe at trot: look for signs of unlevelness, e.g. bobbing of the head and dipping of the hindquarters.
- Observe as the horse is turned away from the handler thus putting more weight on the inside limbs: the horse may take uneven steps.
- Listen to the regularity of the footfalls.
- Shoulder problems are exaggerated when trotting down hill.
- Poor hocks take short stabbing strides, wearing the toe or the shoe quickly and often pushing the shoe back.
- Poor stifles result in a dragging movement with the horse appearing to hesitate before bringing the foot forwards. At rest the horse may stand with a hind leg resting crossed under the body.
- Hip and stifle problems may make the horse stand with stifles and toes pointing out.
- Muscle and ligament problems often get better on exercise but are worse the next day.
- Navicular, ringbone and arthritic problems get worse on exercise.
- Back the horse up, checking that the movement is an even two-time pace.

Ask to see the horse under saddle and perform some specialist movements depending on what you want to do with him after purchase.

- Observe that his breathing and pulse rate recover normally and do not seem excessive for the amount of exercise done.

The horse must also please your eye, be the size, age and type that you want, and perform obediently and correctly for his stage of training.

Breeding or Pedigree

Thoroughbreds can trace their ancestry back for many generations, making it possible to follow and concentrate specific bloodlines. However, competition horses in the UK have only recently started to emerge from the Dark Ages as far as this is concerned! The introduction of continental breeds with their detailed stud books has made British breeders look to their laurels and has led to the introduction of registration and record keeping as demonstrated by the British Warmblood Society. Conformation is highly heritable: look at what man has managed to do to dogs by selective breeding. Temperament will also be inherited as well as being affected by environment. Excellence breeds excellence: sires such as Marius, Nimmerdor and Almé are all proof of this.

2
Equine movement and action

We have discussed the attributes of our ideal equine athlete, which include good conformation and good action. In order to analyse conformation and to understand how it affects a horse's movement we need to look at the horse's skeleton, the muscles attached to the skeleton and how these muscles move the bones to move the horse.

The Skeleton

The skeletal system (Fig. 2.1) includes bones, cartilage and joints and is divided into two parts: the *appendicular* skeleton and the *axial* skeleton. The appendicular skeleton consists of the bones of the limbs, and the axial skeleton is the skull, vertebral column (spine), the ribs and the sternum.

The Axial Skeleton

The spine, the horse's vertebral column, can be divided into five main areas which are identified by the number and shape of the vertebrae.

(1) The neck containing seven *cervical* vertebrae.
(2) The upper back containing 18 *thoracic* vertebrae (Fig. 2.2).
(3) The lower back (loins) containing six *lumbar* vertebrae (Fig. 2.3).
(4) The sacrum containing five fused *sacral* vertebrae.
(5) The tail containing approximately 18 *coccygeal* or *caudal* vertebrae.

Vertebrae have basic features in common but become more specialised in certain areas. They form a long chain which carries the spinal cord. They have spinal, lateral and articular processes, a body and an arch which forms the foramen for the protection of the spinal cord. The spinal and the lateral processes provide a means of attachment for muscles and ligaments. Their job is to carry and protect the spinal cord which carries messages from the brain via the nerves to the rest of the body. The spine transmits the forces of the legs to the body and

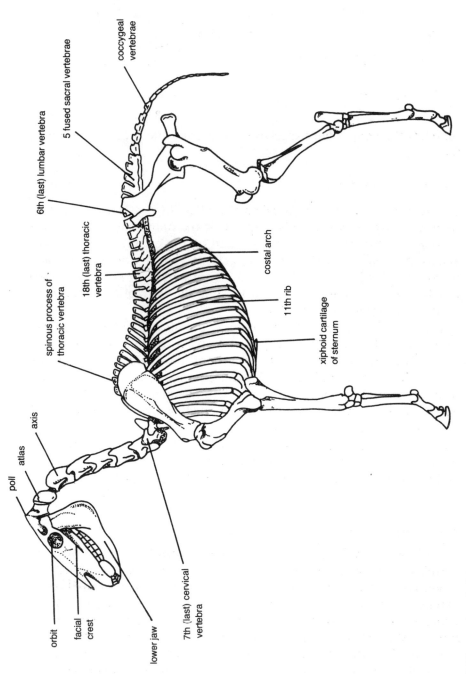

coccygeal
vertebrae

5 fused sacral vertebrae

6th (last) lumbar vertebra

18th (last) thoracic
vertebra

spinous process of
thoracic vertebra

costal arch

11th rib

xiphoid cartilage
of sternum

axis

atlas

poll

orbit

facial
crest

lower jaw

7th (last) cervical
vertebra

Fig. 2.1 The equine skeleton.

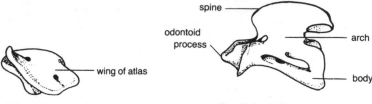

Fig. 2.2 Atlas vertebra.　　　　　*Fig. 2.3* Axis vertebra.

supports the horse's huge digestive system and the pregnant uterus of the mare.

The cervical vertebrae

The first cervical vertebra is called the atlas (Fig. 2.2) and is a short tube with large wings on either side. It is the only vertebra which has no body, and it articulates with the skull on the occipital condyles and allows the head to flex (a nodding action). The second cervical vertebra, the axis (Fig. 2.3), has on the front part the *odontoid* process which extends forwards into the atlas and allows rotation of the head on the neck (from side to side).

The long, strong ligament of the neck, the *nuchal ligament*, attaches to the axis. The nuchal ligament has two parts: the funicular part goes forwards from the withers to the skull and the second part branches in a fan-like formation from the funicular part and radiates downwards to attach to the cervical vertebrae. The ligament helps hold up the horse's very heavy head and neck, and enables the head and the neck to be raised and lowered. The joints between the other cervical vertebrae allow lateral bending and arching of the neck. It is important to note that the vertebrae in the neck form two curves, a higher curve and a lower curve. The curves are deep in the neck and do not follow the crest.

The thoracic vertebrae

The thoracic vertebrae (Fig. 2.4) are typical vertebrae united by intervertebral cartilaginous pads called *discs*. The spinous processes are very large, giving rise to the pronounced withers of the horse and allowing extensive muscle and ligament attachment. The way these spinous processes of the withers are directed is of great importance to the horse and to its ability as an athlete. There are two articulations, one between the discs and the bodies of the vertebrae, and the lateral articulations on each side of the vertebrae. The movement between the thoracic vertebrae in the horse is limited in comparison with that which occurs in many animals.

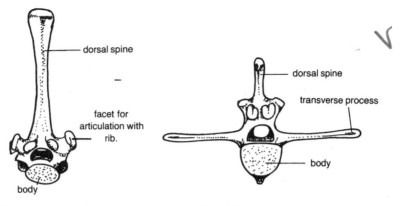

Fig. 2.4 Thoracic vertebra.   *Fig. 2.5* Lumbar vertebra.

The lumbar vertebrae

The lumbar vertebrae (Fig. 2.5) make up the loin region and as with the thoracic vertebrae have a strictly defined and very limited degree of movement. In fact, apart from the neck and tail, the horse's spine shows very little movement. Some movement is found between the last thoracic and the first lumbar vertebrae and between the first three lumbar vertebrae, and there is very strictly limited movement between the hind lumbar vertebrae. The degree of movement depends on the thickness of the intervertebral discs, which are firmly attached to the vertebrae almost like part of the bone that has not yet become calcified. Indeed as the horse ages it is common to find that the discs become calcified thus joining vertebrae together. There may even be further outgrowths of bone acting as bridges across neighbouring bones. Fusion between vertebrae tends to be the rule not the exception in the athletic horse. Sometimes two adjacent lumbar vertebrae may be joined by the transverse processes on one side but not the other causing the horse pain until both sides become fused.

The sacrum

This is a composite bone made up of five vertebrae, situated beneath the loins in the croup region. The pelvic bones are attached to either side of it by the *sacroiliac joint*.

The coccygeal (caudal) vertebrae

These can vary in number from 15 to 21 and decrease progressively in size and complexity from the first to the last.

The total length of the spine is a succession of curves so that it is slightly arched at the upper end of the neck and concave above in the

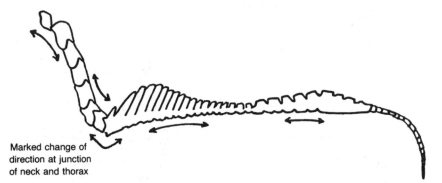

Marked change of
direction at junction
of neck and thorax

Fig. 2.6 The spine is a series of curves.

lower third of the neck (Fig. 2.6). At the junction of the neck and thorax there is a marked change of direction and a gentle curve, concave below, through the thoracic and lumbar regions which helps support the body weight. The dorsal spines of the thorax are bound in a row by strong ligaments.

At walk the spine can be seen to move sideways, but at faster paces there is increased muscular resistance to these forces to minimise any sideways movement of the spine. Vertical forces which tend to increase the curvature of the spine are actively resisted so that the resultant straightening of the thoracolumbar bow adds significantly to the forward propulsive force. Above the spinal column the *longissimus dorsi* muscle and below it the *psoas minor* muscle contract to stop the horse flexing its back. When the synchronisation between these muscles fails, for example in a fall, the back becomes susceptible to fracture.

The ribs

Each of the 18 thoracic vertebrae carries a pair of ribs. There are eight pairs of true or sternal ribs which are directly attached to the sternum or breastbone; the remainder are false ribs and are not attached to the sternum. Ribs contain spongy red bone marrow and are important throughout the life of the horse as red blood cell forming organs; they also carry the muscles that control breathing. The first rib carries the nerves of the *brachial plexus* which transmits sensory and locomotory information to the forelimb. If the first rib is broken it can lead to radial paralysis or dropped elbow.

The sternum

The sternum or breast bone is a keel-shaped bone in the centre of the chest that supports the true ribs.

The Appendicular Skeleton

The appendicular skeleton is attached to the axial skeleton by the pelvic (hip) girdle and pectoral (shoulder) girdle. The pectoral girdle is incomplete in horses, consisting of only a scapula or shoulder blade, so the fore limb is attached to the body by muscle and tendon rather than by the clavicle or collar bone as in the human. The pelvic girdle usually consists of three pairs of bones, the ilium, ischium and pubis. It connects the hind limbs to the body by a ball-and-socket joint, and is in turn attached to the spinal column at the sacrum.

The fore limb

A strong bony attachment is not necessary for the fore limb (Fig. 2.7) because it functions more to support the body than to propel it. This arrangement of muscle attachment also allows greater absorption of concussion.

The scapula. This bone serves to attach the fore limb to the trunk by muscles and to transmit motions of the fore limb to the body. The scapulae are flattened bones designed to glide backwards and forwards over the ribs and to allow the trunk to move between them. In other words the thorax of the horse is slung between the shoulderblades giving a freedom of movement not allowed by the inflexible spine. A long scapula gives a horse a sloping shoulder, and a long stride and a free action of the front limbs.

The humerus. This bone connects the scapula and the rest of the limb and acts as the origin and point of insertion of major muscles that control the upper and lower parts of the fore limb. Its angular arrangement between the shoulderblades and the rest of the legs allows it to act as a shock-absorbing device to cushion the impact of the hooves against the ground.

The radius and ulna. These bones are fused in the horse so that there is no rotation of the limb and movement is restricted to a backward and forward action designed for propulsion. The ulna is very small apart from the *olecranon process* — the bony part of the elbow. The elbow joint is known as a *hinge joint* or *ginglymus*, and only allows movement in one direction.

The knee or carpus (Fig. 2.8). This is a group of eight small bones which corresponds to the human wrist. The knee functions both as a hinge joint and as a shock-absorbing device; the combined movement of its joints forms a major area of flexion which transmits forward movement to the body and contributes to the length of the stride. Hairline fractures of these small carpal bones can be a major problem in young racehorses.

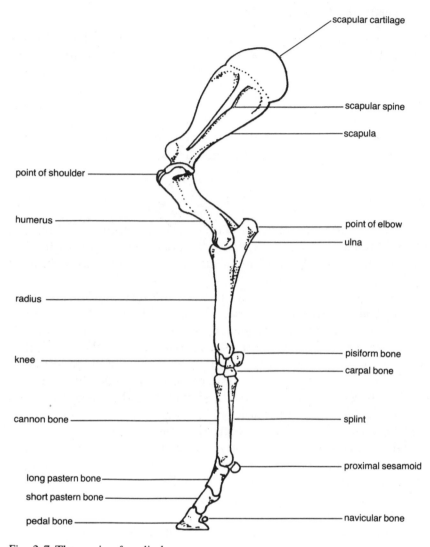

Fig. 2.7 The equine fore limb.

The metacarpals. Only three metacarpals are present in the horse, the cannon and two splint bones. The splint bones help support the knee but they are not weight bearing because they finish about two-thirds down the shaft of the cannon bone.

The phalanges. These are the long and short pastern bones and the pedal bone, and are equivalent to the human finger.

The digital sesamoid bones. There are three sesamoid bones, two proximal, commonly known as the sesamoids, and one distal, the nav-

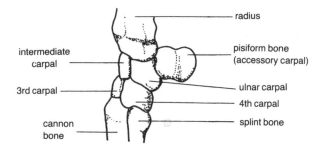

Fig. 2.8 The horse's knee.

icular bone. These bones allow muscles to exert greater pull on the moveable bones nearer the end of the limb. They give the tendons which ride over them greater leverage and are very important to give force and power to the stride, improve muscle efficiency and increase speed.

The hind limb

The hind limb (Fig. 2.9) has a bony attachment to the spine so that the propulsive forces and concussion are transmitted directly to the spine.

The pelvic girdle (Fig. 2.10). This consists of two equal halves, the pelvic bones, welded together, plus the sacrum and first three coccygeal vertebrae. Each half of the pelvis consists of three flat bones; the upper portion which is attached to the sacrum is called the *ilium*. The front portion of the pelvic floor between the hind limbs is the *pubis* and the hindmost portion is the *ischium*. The three bones meet at a cup-shaped cavity called the *acetabulum* which articulates with the head of the femur. The ilium is the largest portion and has a triangular shape, the outermost angle of which is called the *tuber coxae* — the hip bone. This is joined to the sacrum by the *sacroiliac ligament* giving rise to the croup area. The ilium provides an extensive area for muscle attachment.

The hip joint. The joint between the pelvis and the femur permits movement in every direction, giving a great range of directional movement which is limited in its extent compared, for example, with that in the dog. The hind feet of the horse rarely extend forwards beyond a line dropped from its navel. Compare this with the movement in the greyhound, the hind feet of which may land level to the point of its shoulder. The femur also helps to protect the organs contained within the pelvis, it connects the pelvis to the rest of the hind limb, it serves as the origin and point of insertion of many major muscles, and it gives

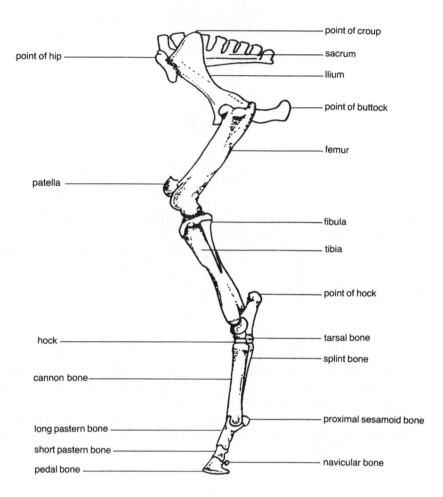

point of hip

point of croup

sacrum

Ilium

point of buttock

femur

patella

fibula

tibia

point of hock

hock

tarsal bone

splint bone

cannon bone

proximal sesamoid bone

long pastern bone

short pastern bone

pedal bone

navicular bone

Fig. 2.9 The equine hind limb.

a positive connection between the hind legs and the spine giving an efficient transfer of propulsive force to the body.

The patella. This sesamoid bone and the joint between the femur and tibia make up the stifle joint which is equivalent to the human knee. The design allows maximum application of muscle power to extend the upper hind limb giving great drive and speed of movement.

The tibia and fibula. The fibula of the horse is practically vestigial. The tibia connects the stifle to the hock.

The hock or tarsus (Fig. 2.11). This joint consists of six or seven short bones arranged in two rows. The first and second tarsal bones are usually fused. The largest bone at the back of the hock has a long

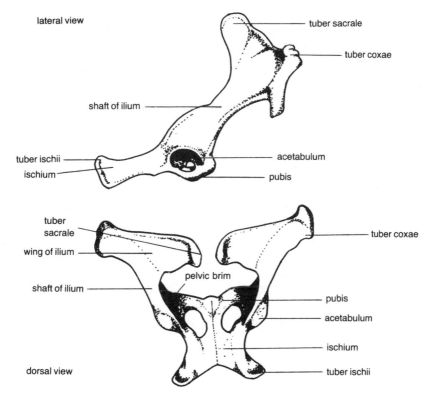

Fig. 2.10 Pelvis of the horse.

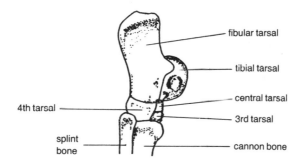

Fig. 2.11 The horse's hock.

bony process called the *tuber calcis*, and the *achilles tendon* of the *gastrocnemius* muscle attaches here. The hock is a locomotion and shock absorption device and gives a high degree of leverage to the hind foot.

The metatarsals and digits. These correspond to the bones in the front leg.

Skeletal Muscle

Skeletal muscle is made up of long fibres which in turn consist of many microscopic *myofibrils* — the basic unit which is responsible for the contractile properties of muscle (Fig. 2.12). Each group of myofibrils is gathered together in a bunch and covered in connective tissue to make a muscle fibre. Fibres combine to make a muscle bundle which gives coarseness or 'grain' to the muscle; muscle bundles are gathered together to make up the muscle itself. Muscle usually consists of a body and two ends which finish in tough connective tissue cords called tendons that attach it to the skeleton. Muscles in the leg are usually arranged in *antagonistic pairs*. In other words, for every muscle that performs one action, there is another that does the opposite. For example, in humans the biceps of the upper arm flexes the elbow joint and the triceps extends the joint. Skeletal muscle is rarely completely relaxed, resulting in muscle tone. That is, the slight contraction in one

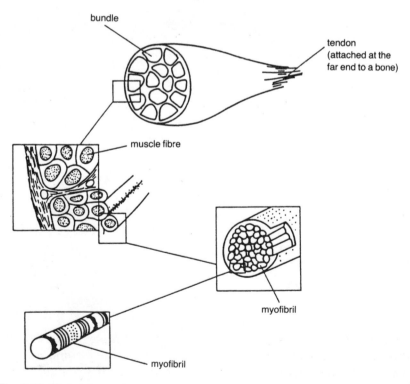

Fig. 2.12 Skeletal muscle.

muscle of an antagonistic pair is counterbalanced by slight contraction in the other muscle and hence the body is ready to give an instant response. Muscle lacking tone will eventually become useless.

The Role of Muscle in Locomotion (Figs 2.13 and 2.14)

The shoulderblade of the horse is supported in a sling of muscle and connective tissue and attached to the body by a large muscle, the *serratus* muscle. Contraction of the front or anterior part of the serratus pulls the scapula forwards, and contraction of the rear part pulls the shoulderblade back. However, it is the *brachiocephalicus* that is responsible for most shoulder movement. This is a long, flattened muscle arising behind the ear, passing down the whole length of the neck and inserting on to the humerus. This means that the horse moves more freely in front when the head is held high or fully extended, and riding on a tight rein or with a fixed martingale impairs the horse's movement. The degree of development of the brachiocephalicus is an important indicator when assessing the fitness of a horse. When the horse's head is advanced and the neck is held firmly by its own muscles, contraction

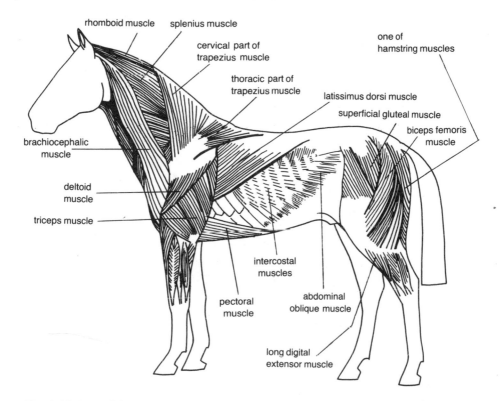

Fig. 2.13 Superficial muscle.

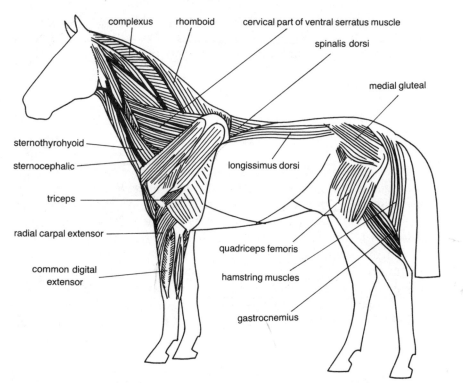

Fig. 2.14 Deep muscles.

of the brachiocephalicus carries the arm and knee forwards. When the horse is standing still, it turns its head by contraction of the brachiocephalicus. The *triceps* and *biceps* extend and flex the elbow joint while the upper part of the shoulder is connected to the body by the *trapezius* muscles which form a sling over the neck and withers. The hoof is moved by the muscles of the forearm which act through long tendons to the lower limb. The muscles of the shoulders act as weight supporters and shock absorbers: two-thirds of the horse's bodyweight is carried on the forehand, and the scapula should incline well backwards at the upper end to give good stride length and to provide absorption of concussion. The sling of muscles carrying the horse's body between its shoulderblades allows the chest of the horse to rise and fall between the shoulders and to lean to one side or the other without the forelegs having to move from the perpendicular.

The Centre of Gravity (see Fig. 1.1)

There is a lot of talk in the dressage world about the horse's centre of gravity and how it moves as the horse's degree of training advances.

The centre of gravity is the point at which the horse's mass is evenly balanced. Due to the horse's conformation, i.e. with two-thirds of the bodyweight on the forehand, the centre of gravity in the standing horse is nearer the shoulders than the hips. This enables the horse to rest its hind feet without losing its balance. Each individual horse's centre of gravity will vary according to its conformation, weight distribution and attitude. For example, raising the head pushes the centre of gravity backwards. In order to raise a foreleg, the centre of gravity must first be moved back so the horse raises its head and neck; contraction of the *serratus ventralis* then raises the thorax on the side on which the muscles are acting, throwing extra weight on to this foreleg and relieving the opposite foreleg of enough weight to permit the elbow to flex and the joint to be moved forwards. Contraction of the *anterior deep pectorals* (between the front legs) also raises the thorax so that there is flexion of the hocks while the hind feet are still firmly on the ground. This flexion may be almost imperceptible, but a drop of an inch or so of the hindquarters may release 20 to 100 kg from the forehand, moving the centre of gravity backwards.

Movement of the Front Limbs

In order to lift a forefoot, not only does the centre of gravity have to move back but also the shoulder and elbow have to flex. Shoulder flexion involves the *deltoids*, *teres minor* and *teres major*. Elbow flexion involves contraction of the biceps and relaxation of the triceps. The knee moves forwards and upwards, raising the foot from the ground. Flexors at the back of the knee contract to flex the knee and digital joints. The foot is now suspended from the withers by the *dorsal scapular ligaments* and the *trapezius*. The limb is brought forwards by the brachiocephalicus (which pulls the humerus forwards) and the serratus ventralis (thoracic part) which pulls the scapula down and back. As the leg is lifted it is folded; excessive shoe weight or hoof length will increase the amount of folding. Consequently racehorses are shod with light plates whereas hackneys have heavy shoes. After the leg has advanced enough it is straightened; the shoulder joint is extended by the *supraspinatus* and the elbow joint by the *triceps*. The knee, coffin, pastern and fetlock joints move into extension by contraction of carpal and digital extensors. As retraction of the leg begins, the common extensor muscles slacken and the tendons of the lower leg align the coffin and pastern joints (ready for hitting the ground) so that the limb is rigid as it hits the ground. As the foot is firmly placed on the ground it acts as a fixed fulcrum. The impetus of the body turning above the foot actually drives the body forwards. When the foot is on the ground, the shoulder and elbow are fixed by contraction of the biceps and triceps. The *latissimus dorsi* and *deep pectorals* pull the humerus back, and the serratus ventralis (cervical part), *rhomboideus* and *deep pectorals* pull the upper end of the scapula forwards and the body rotates forwards on the rigid leg. Actual propulsive force occurs when the shoulder has moved on past the level of the hoof. When the foot is on the ground, the fetlock sinks. This movement is controlled by the suspensory ligament, then the superficial digital flexor tendon, then the deep flexor tendon and finally the check ligament. These tendons and ligaments help to reduce shock and add smoothness to the action. The fetlock is extended so that the digits are in a straight line with the leg when the foot lands; it then overextends and recovers after the leg passes over the vertical. In this way the limb is shortened and lengthened, helping to keep the body at nearly the same level throughout its stride. The straightening or recovery of the fetlock adds forward propulsive force to the stride and is helped by the elasticity of the suspensory ligament. Powerful deep flexor muscles pull the pedal bone back with such energy that the rotation of the coffin joint and upward movement of the fetlock give propulsive force to the leg. When the hoof leaves the ground, the triceps relaxes and the elastic recoil of the biceps tendon pulls the humerus forwards. The rhomboideus and serratus ventralis (cervical) are relaxing, allowing elastic rebound of the serratus ventralis (thoracic).

The Stay Mechanism

Horses are able to relax in a standing position due to the stay mechanism, a system of muscles and ligaments that firmly locks the main joints in position. This system is based on the suspensory apparatus of the limb; the suspensory ligament running down the back of the cannon bone divides into two branches inserted into the proximal sesamoid bones (Fig. 2.15) preventing overextension of the fetlock. The superficial and deep digital flexor tendons supplement the action of the suspensory ligament and are in turn supported by the check ligament. The latter is unusual in that it runs from bone to tendon and makes the tendon function as a ligament by cutting off the muscle attachment above. Thus as the body weight presses down through the fetlock the suspensory ligament tightens followed by the flexor tendons. The stay mechanism is also helped by the serratus ventralis muscle which contains inelastic fibrous tissue that supports the body when the muscles are relaxed. The weight of the body is hanging from the upper end of the scapula, which tends to close the shoulder joint. This closing is resisted by the biceps (which attaches the scapula to the radius), which in turn must be prevented from flexing the elbow so that the leg remains rigid; this is accomplished by the triceps. Shoulder flexion is

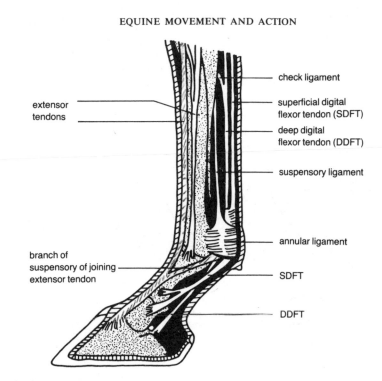

check ligament

extensor
tendons

superficial digital
flexor tendon (SDFT)

deep digital
flexor tendon (DDFT)

suspensory ligament

annular ligament

branch of
suspensory of joining
extensor tendon

SDFT

DDFT

Fig. 2.15 Ligaments and tendons of the lower limbs.

prevented by the supraspinatus muscle. The knee is prevented from buckling forwards by the tendon running from the biceps.

Movement of the Hind Leg

Movement of the hind leg is different because it has a direct connection to the axial skeleton. The femur is extended by a group of large *gluteal* muscles and the *biceps femoris*, and it is flexed by the *quadriceps femoris*. The gluteal muscles also extend the hip joint and flex the stifle joint. Flexion of the hip joint is necessary to carry the femur and stifle forwards; the stifle is also flexed, which in turn causes hock flexion. The superficial flexor flexes the joints of the lower limb but when the foot hits the ground the hind leg is locked into a rigid spoke; muscles pull the rigid leg backwards and strongly stabilise the stifle and hock joints. The limb is turned on the head of the femur, extending the hip joint. As the limb approaches the vertical, the stifle and hock flex slightly and the fetlocks sink to act as shock absorbers. The stifle is actively extended by the quadriceps muscles acting on the patella, and the rump and hamstring muscles extend the hip, stifle and hock.

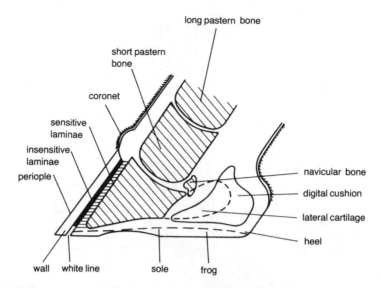

Fig. 2.16 The structure of the foot, showing the digital cushion and lateral cartilage.

Landing on the Hoof

At rest the horse's weight is taken on the wall of the hoof and the frog. The weight acts down to the tip of the pedal bone but is spread among thousands of sensitive laminae. The plates of tissue are attached to the periosteum covering the pedal bone, and interdigitate with insensitive laminae originating from the inside of the hoof wall (Fig. 2.16). During movement the horse lands on its heels first and then the quarters and toe of the hoof. At impact the heels spread as weight is passed down the bones of the leg to the digital cushion and frog. The digital cushion is compressed and presses against the lateral cartilages thus causing the heels of the hoof to spread; obviously this effect is limited in the shod horse. The lateral cartilages also press against blood vessels and send blood back up the leg. At the same time blood is trapped in the complicated blood vessels of the foot, acting as a hydraulic cushion for the pedal bone and absorbing concussion.

Joints

Joints are formed when two or more bones come together (Fig. 2.17), and are held bound together by bands of flexible but inelastic fibrous tissue called ligaments. *Diarthrodial* joints are movable and can be classified by their action, e.g. gliding, hinge, pivot or ball-and-socket

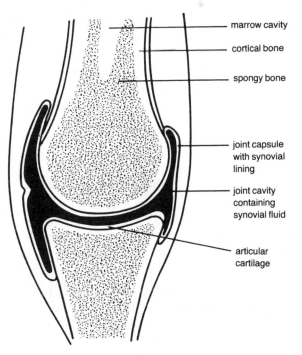

Fig. 2.17 The structure of a joint.

joint. Gliding movement occurs between the processes of cervical vertebrae which slide over each other. Angular movement occurs in the elbow joint: in flexion the angle diminishes whereas in extension the angle increases. Joint movement which allows the movement of a limb towards the median plane is adduction; abduction is movement of the limb away from the middle line.

Tendons and Ligaments

Tendons have several very important functions in the horse:

- They transfer muscle activity to bone.
- They act as an amplifier during rapid muscle contraction.
- They are an elastic energy store.
- They absorb unexpected movement.

Tendons are formed by an extension of the connective tissue membrane which encloses muscle, and they become firmly attached to bone by becoming continuous with the membrane covering the bone (periosteum). Tendon is made up of dense white fibrous connective tissue which is arranged as long parallel fibres giving great tensile strength and some degree of elasticity. These fibres are made of a protein called collagen type I; bundles of type I fibres are bound together by the *enotenon membrane* and the whole tendon is surrounded by the *epitenon*. The tendon is enclosed by the *tendon sheath* at sites of friction. This sheath increases the capacity of the tendon to slide freely over bones and joints. The sheath consists of two layers with lubricating fluid between them. The inner layer which is connected with the epitenon is smooth, and the outer layer is connected to the surrounding tissues to hold the tendon in place. Blood vessels and nerves enter the tendon via the sheath. Inside the tendon the parallel collagen fibres are interspersed with cells called *fibroblasts* which produce *tropocollagen* which in turn gives rise to *collagen*. The collagen is regularly renewed and replaced because each fibre has a limited lifespan: it can only contract and expand a set number of times. The tendon will not withstand the stress of taking the horse's weight if it can no longer stretch and relax. Stress is particularly high when the muscles are tired and can no longer act as shock absorbers. Then all the strain gets placed on the tendon, and tendon fibres tear giving the characteristic signs of tendon injury. The risk of tendon injury can be avoided to a certain extent by correct fittening. Repeated loading of the tendon during slow work at the beginning of a fitness programme tends to make the tendon more elastic by stimulating greater turnover of collagen so that each fibre is younger and consequently has more 'crimp' which allows expansion in length. 'Crimp' describes the arrangement of the collagen fibres within the tendon. They have a wavy form which can be pulled straight allowing a 3% increase in tendon length. Blood supply to the tendons of the horse's lower leg is very limited but vital; blood brings oxygen, and if there is a lack of oxygen there will be insufficient numbers of fibroblasts to replace all the collagen that is worn out during work. Thus the tendon gradually degenerates and becomes weaker, eventually resulting in acute tendon damage.

Locomotion: How a Horse Moves

Having looked at the scientific aspects behind our horse's movement we can now look at locomotion from the point of view of our equine athlete.

How do we know if our horse's movement can be improved, and what criteria are needed to give us the correct information? How can we assess and monitor our improvements? How does the horse put its foot down, and what part receives the greatest strain in each phase of movement? What can affect the movement? How can we prolong the horse's usefulness? How can we maintain fitness? These questions show how important it is to understand the movement of your horse so you can judge, assess, improve and monitor your horse and collect information for your horse's profile.

The ideal athlete will move with economy of energy. He will be light and balanced. His action will be free from discomfort or stiffness. He will have good coordination and exhibit no compensations in his movement patterns, and show minimum change in movement patterns when fatigued.

Gait analysis can be used to monitor gait characteristics on a day-to-day basis to show how your horse differs from the ideal so that appropriate modification can be made in training and preparation for competitions. Subclinical unlevelness can be detected before serious breakdown occurs, and appropriate action can be taken to prevent breakdown.

The study of locomotion involves *biomechanics*, which is the investigation of how internal and external forces affect living bodies. Scientists divide biomechanics into two main areas, biostatics and biodynamics. Biostatics involves the body systems at rest, when the forces acting on the body are balanced, and the study of the body tissues which are involved with movement, i.e. muscles, tendons, bones and ligaments. Biodynamics is when the forces on the body are unbalanced resulting in movement.

The Stride

During locomotion the horse's limbs undergo repeated cycles of movement which can be divided into different phases. The *stance phase* occurs when the limb is in contact with the ground, and the *swing phase* when the limb is being carried though the air.

In the *stance phase*, in other words when the horse's leg is on the ground, the limb undergoes two different kinds of stress, concussion and compression. Both these stresses will be affected by conformation, shoeing and trimming, the speed of the gait, the rider, the surface, and the fitness and development of the horse. As previously described, the heel of the foot hits the ground first and anything that interferes with placement of the foot will cause stress and strain. Both sides of the foot should contact the ground simultaneously, and as the full weight falls on the foot the knee and foot bones take most of the strain. If the horse's weight falls unevenly due to its conformation or the going, the uneven strain can cause injury.

The *swing phase* is the forward reach or protraction of the limb followed by the body's moving forwards, which appears as if the limb is being retracted or moving back. After the foot has contacted the ground, the horse's bodyweight passes over the limb on the ground. The heel leaves the ground before the toe, an interval called the *break-*

over time. From the time the hoof contacts the ground to *midstance*, when the horse's bodyweight is positioned directly over the limb, there is a deceleration or braking phase followed by an acceleration or propulsion phase from midstance to take-off as the toe pushes off. A complete cycle of these movements is called a stride.

We can measure the stride length and other movement parameters such as the path and direction the footprints make; and determine whether the stride is balanced and there is flexion of the joints. We will call this *step and stride* monitoring. Details on how to do this will be given in the next chapter and will be another way of assessing and monitoring your horse's progress. There are several definitions of step and stride. The one used here is that which is normally used in biomechanical and anatomy studies. Remember: the stride length is from placement to placement of the same foot, and the stride is divided into two as it passes the opposite limb at midstance, giving an *anterior step* and a *posterior step* to the stride.

We can also measure the *step width*. If the horse is reasonably straight in his development and of average conformation, the total length of the stride of each limb should be the same. However, the steps — that is, both the *anterior* and the *posterior* elements — can give different measurements. The difference between step measurements may indicate that the horse is either delaying putting his foot down (delaying the stance phase) or delaying lifting his foot (delaying the swing phase) There are many reasons for not placing the heels down with confidence, or wishing to put the foot down as quickly as possible: muscle imbalance or muscle weakness, tack problems, pending over-use soreness, shoeing and trimming problems, faults in or difficulties being experienced by the rider, the start of more serious problems, or a horse returning to work after some period of lameness.

If a base measurement is established for your horse this will be a standard with which future measurements can be compared, and subsequent monitoring can be added to your horse's profile. This is very informative and can indicate very slight problems developing long before any visual signs can be seen or heat felt. If these early warnings are ignored and work goes on as usual, in a week or two problems will come to light (in the form of heat and swelling in the tendons, splints and ligaments for example), which can take the horse out of work for some time. Tissue injury like this can cause long-term weakness. However, if work is stopped or reduced as soon as any deviations in the measurements show, you may catch the problem before the tissue is too badly damaged.

Subsequent measurements can monitor the degree of healing, and the work programme can be adjusted accordingly. Step and stride measurements can be used to monitor a horse's increased fitness and muscle development during his fittening programme, and again will give an early indication of such problems as incorrect movement and development. Assessing your horse's fitness after injury is very important because the horse is only as strong as his weakest point — in other words the healed injury and any compensations he developed while coping with his altered gait patterns. The healed injury means that the horse needs to undergo a fittening or rehabilitation programme to rebalance him. Gait fatigue is the main cause of more serious breakdown, and monitoring the gait patterns can give you guidelines on how much work the horse can do before fatigue of the unfit part begins to alter his timing.

If you have kept records of your horse's step and stride in your profile for some time and they have been very consistent but then start to show changes, it could indicate that changes are taking place in the feet or legs. This would enable you to seek veterinary treatment before lameness becomes apparent, and would give the vet information on which to base more detailed diagnostic tests. Your farrier may also be pleased to know of any variation occurring in the feet. Deteriorating step and stride measurements have even been known to show that a saddle needs repairing, or that a rider had not recovered from a fall and was upsetting the horse's action.

Before we look at how to measure the step and stride for our profiles, we must be sure of what 'good movement' is. We have already stated that conformation in terms of the skeletal shape and developed shape will affect movement. Good conformation helps the horse move well.

Before looking at walk, trot, canter, gallop and the rein back in detail, a few terms which we will meet should be defined. This should be helpful since there appears to be some confusion of definitions depending on the discipline in which the horse is involved and the common or specific usage of the particular terms.

Rhythm is the regularity of the foot falls. *Tempo* is used in two ways, the speed of the rhythm within each gait or the velocity of the gait. *Velocity* is the product of stride length and stride frequency, in other words speed. *Cadence* in gait analysis refers to the number of foot strikes per minute. In dressage terms it describes the rhythm with impulsion and activity. On *two tracks* the horse is moving forwards straight, each lateral pair of limbs making its own track. In other words the right hind follows the right fore and the left hind follows the left fore.

Path denotes the direction and any deviation of the footprints from a straight line, the width of the placement and the tracks formed. Different types of conformation and degree of development are taken into consideration when analysing these path patterns for straightness, equal weight, way of placing the foot and, on a harder surface, the

sound of the hoof beats; for example, at the walk we should hear four
firm beats.

Flight of the limb indicates the height and position of the limbs in
relation to each other during the stride. *Placement* is how the horse
places each of his feet on the ground, the period of time the foot stays
on the ground, the weight on the foot and any scuffing, sliding or twisting of the foot.

The Walk (Fig. 2.18)

The walk is a symmetrical gait. The horse's feet follow one another in
the following sequence: off hind, off fore, near hind, near fore, giving
a four-time beat. The rhythm should be even and regular. The way
the horse walks says a great deal about his biomechanics and athletic
ability, about the way he has been developed and ridden and perhaps
about his temperament. The horse that strides out willingly, with his
shoulders swinging forwards, his hind feet overstepping his front feet,
and reaching forwards under himself and engaging his quarters, is a
promising picture. The degree of overstepping will depend on conformation and development: A long hind limb giving the horse a huge
stride will suggest that he can gallop well but may have problems giving
a regular walk, particularly when collected. The length of a stride is
usually between 5 ft 6 in and 6 ft (168–183 cm).

In the walk at least two feet are in contact with the ground at any
one time. Assessing the walk, it is important to think of eight different
movements (two times four) as it is possible for a horse to have four
regular beats followed by four irregular beats. With a well developed
horse, movement should start from behind. The horse in turn stands
on three legs, right fore, left hind, left fore, then the two left lateral
legs, and again on three legs, left hind, left fore and right hind, and
then two diagonal legs, right hind and left fore. The whole process is
repeated again with the opposite legs: standing on three legs, right
hind, right fore, left hind, then the two right laterals and again on three
legs, left hind, right hind and right fore, and the two diagonal legs, left
hind and right fore. The purity and regularity of the walk should be
judged throughout the eight different movements. The intervals when
the legs are raised from the ground and then returned to the ground
should be of exactly the same duration for each leg, be it a lateral or
diagonal leg.

The walk is an essential part of the fitness programme and is a very
good form of exercise provided it is carried out in a balanced, rhyth-
mic, swinging and energetic manner. Many horses fail to develop well
as their walking exercise is an unbalanced, unenergetic shuffle or is too
hurried and unbalanced. The walk is a gait at which the horse uses a

vast number of muscles without putting them under stress. The muscles contract and relax regularly encouraging good circulation. In an active walk the back of the horse is pulsating and swinging. This will help to remove tension and muscle bunching which can restrict the circulation. The walk is often used as a rest and relaxation after or between other more strenuous movements.

It is useful to assess a horse at walk as a lot of imperfections can show up. However, the trot is a better gait to assess a horse that has a lameness. The walk will be influenced by conformation, levels of development and training, rider ability, past injuries and incorrect development. The walk in dressage terms has four variations, free, collected, medium and extended, and each has certain criteria which must be met to achieve the necessary degree of excellence. Such criteria as lightness, good regular rhythm, obedience, confidence, absence of resistance to the demands of the rider, and active engagement of the hind limbs must be met.

The Trot (Fig. 2.19)

The trot is a two-time gait and the legs move in diagonal pairs (near hind, off fore and off hind and near fore) with a period of suspension when all the limbs are off the ground; one fore limb is protracting while the other is retracting, and the opposite occurs in the hind limbs.

The period of suspension is the part when the rider is usually rising out of the saddle. The longer this phase, the more difficult or fatiguing for the rider which is relevant for long-distance riders.

Four variations of the trot are recognised in dressage, collected, working, medium and extended. When analysing the trot, the steps and the stride length should be equal within each variation of the trot. The length of stride in the trot is 8–9 ft (2.4–3 m) and the rate of the trot can range between 8 and 11 mph (13–17 kph).

The placement of the feet should be definite with no sliding of the feet. The path of the feet should be as straight as possible with equal weight on each foot.

The trot should be light and elastic, with the knees and the hocks flexing freely at the same height. There should be no dragging of the toes, and the horse should be balanced and the rhythm the same on the straight and on the circle. A good trot depends on a supple back, good balance, engagement of the hindquarters and elastic and supple joints. The stifles should not turn out but give good clearance as well as support and weight carrying. The hind feet must be placed firmly to give good support and drive. The fore limbs should be placed down lightly without any snapping of the knees or any jarring action. The trot is considered incorrect when the two support legs do not hit the ground together. Usually the hind limb is in advance of the fore limb.

Although the walk is good for assessing and monitoring your horse's development and for picking up early warning signals, it is at the trot that the horse is assessed for lameness. During trot there should be four equal weight-bearing strides in a short time. Many lameness problems are only visible at the trot.

The Canter (Fig. 2.20)

The canter is an asymmetrical gait of three time. If cantering to the right, the sequence of the foot falls is left hind, left fore and right hind together, right fore, followed by a moment of suspension with all feet off the ground before the next stride. A good canter is light, with regular strides, good rhythm and balance. The hindquarters should be correctly engaged, shown by the horse carrying the hind limbs with adequate joint flexion and placing each hind foot on the ground firmly with no hesitation.

A *disunited canter* is incorrect, and occurs when the forehand is on one lead and the hind on another. *Counter canter* is used as an exercise to supple the shoulders and the back. The rider asks the horse to lead with outside fore limb instead of the inside; on a circle to the left the horse is cantering with the right lead.

The following canters are recognised in dressage terms: collected, working, medium and extended. There is increased flexion of the lumbosacral joint at the canter and the gallop.

The Gallop

The gallop is a fast asymmetrical gait of four beats. The sequence of limb placement is non-lead hind, non-lead fore and lead fore, followed by a period of suspension. Inspiration and expiration in the gallop are related to the stride (Fig. 2.21).

Jumping (Fig. 2.22)

All gaits and movements will improve with the correct progressive development. This means with correct work, ensuring that the horse is working within his capacity and is in rhythm and balance at all times. He should improve the elasticity of his movements, be able to carry himself better, produce greater engagement of his quarters and lighten his forehand, and be safer and more competent and confident. If a young horse is asked to jump before his body has developed adequately, he will feel the strain. Although this may not cause visible injury, he may lose confidence and willingness to jump. If a horse loses his will-

Fig. 2.18 The sequence of foot falls at walk.

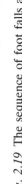

Fig. 2.19 The sequence of foot falls at trot.

Fig. 2.20 The sequence of foot falls at canter (left lead).

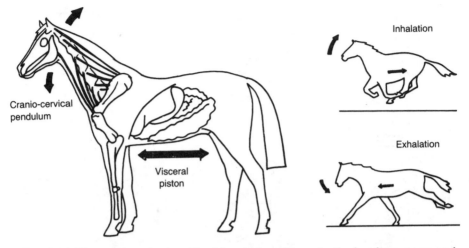

Inhalation

Cranio-cervical
pendulum

Exhalation

Visceral
piston

Fig. 2.21 The synchronisation of stride and breathing. As the head moves up and the gut back the horse breathes in; the head moves down as the horse lands, the gut moves forwards and the horse breathes out.

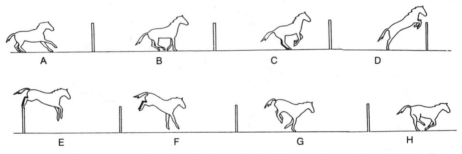

A   B   C   D

E   F   G   H

Fig. 2.22 The jump: A–D, takeoff phase; E–F, airborne phase; G and H, landing phase.

ingness to jump, he may rush through the jump or gallop over it but he will not jump correctly.

Jumping is not a natural thing for the horse to do. We would find it difficult to keep them in fields if it were. The rigidity of the equine spine compared with that of animals that jump naturally, his huge gut and his big head do not help the horse to be an efficient jumper. Showjumpers come in many different types, and all the conformation factors that are important to any equine athlete must be considered: equal proportions, symmetrical balance and the position of the centre of mass, the last being perhaps the most important factor in his ability to negotiate his fences.

The most important factors determining what makes the horse jump best will of course depend on the type of jumping he is asked to do. The hurdler or the steeplechaser will 'gallop leap' over fences: the better he can do this leap within his gallop the less time will he lose and the less stress will he cause to himself. The showjumper on the other hand has to jump his fences and jump them clear, and negotiate a twisting course of fences, each fence needing a different speed of approach and different take-off and landing techniques. Some experts would say that in showjumping it is the athletic ability of the horse on the ground to arrive and position himself at the jump and his recovery after landing that are more important than his ability over a fence. One horse may have more natural ability and the other a taught ability. Whatever it is, the horse must want to jump.

The jump itself is divided into three phases, *take-off*, the *airborne* phase and *landing*. The take-off phase includes the stance phase of the foot just before the jump. The non-lead fore limb begins the take-off and it ends at the lift-off of the lead hind limb: this is now the airborne phase. Impact is when the non-lead front limb brings the horse to the landing phase. This ends in the lift-off of the lead fore limb.

The fore limbs determine the upward thrust of the forehand, and the hindquarters rotate under the body so that they are placed nearer to the fence than the fore limbs. The hind limbs are not placed down quite together, and they do not leave the ground quite together. However, they appear to be used more in unison in showjumping than in the speed jumping of the racehorse. The forehand is already elevated before the hind limbs touch the ground before take-off, and influences the trajectory through the air. The hind limbs increase the upwards impulsion. The trajectory, impulsion and speed together determine the flight over the jump. Most of the joints in the forehand and the hind limbs are flexed as the horse is propelled over the jump. The hind limbs can be flexed to bring the limbs under the body or extended behind.

The classic parabola over a jump occurs when the horse rounds his back and reaches to get over the jump. The more he can use his back, shoulders and hips the better. The less he uses his limbs in flexion the higher he must lift his body over the fence. A good showjumper uses his limb flexion to full advantage. On landing the fore limbs act as struts and the hind limbs are brought down under the body independently, not as a pair.

Since the shape of the bones and the development of the muscles influence the way the horse moves, it is essential that a study is made of the names and positions of the bones in the skeleton, the bones and ligaments which make up the joints, the movements possible in the different joints, and the names and action of the main muscles. This will take a little time to learn but will be of great value to you. Tables 2.1–2.6 will help you to do this. The first row shows the name and lo-

Table 2.1 Neck–withers.

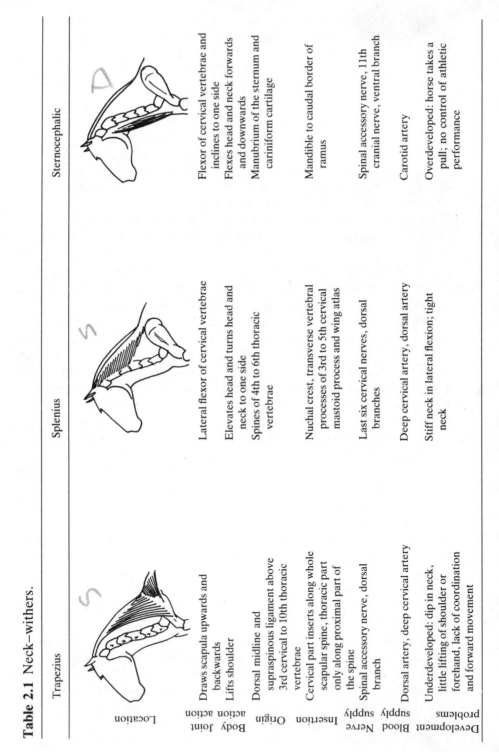

	Trapezius	Splenius	Sternocephalic
Location			
Body action / Joint action	Draws scapula upwards and backwards Lifts shoulder	Lateral flexor of cervical vertebrae Elevates head and turns head and neck to one side	Flexor of cervical vertebrae and inclines to one side Flexes head and neck forwards and downwards
Origin	Dorsal midline and supraspinous ligament above 3rd cervical to 10th thoracic vertebrae	Spines of 4th to 6th thoracic vertebrae	Manubrium of the sternum and cariniform cartilage
Insertion	Cervical part inserts along whole scapular spine, thoracic part only along proximal part of the spine	Nuchal crest, transverse vertebral processes of 3rd to 5th cervical mastoid process and wing atlas	Mandible to caudal border of ramus
Nerve supply	Spinal accessory nerve, dorsal branch	Last six cervical nerves, dorsal branches	Spinal accessory nerve, 11th cranial nerve, ventral branch
Blood supply	Dorsal artery, deep cervical artery	Deep cervical artery, dorsal artery	Carotid artery
Development problems	Underdeveloped: dip in neck, little lifting of shoulder or forehand, lack of coordination and forward movement	Stiff neck in lateral flexion; tight neck	Overdeveloped: horse takes a pull; no control of athletic performance

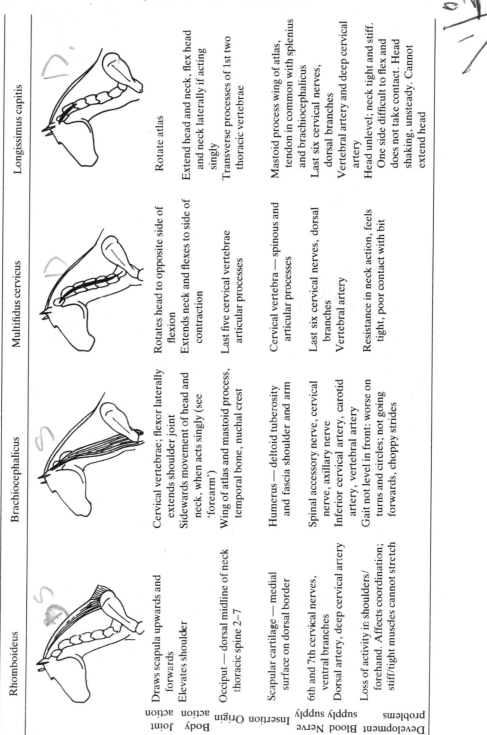

	Rhomboideus	Brachiocephalicus	Multifidus cervicus	Longissimus capitis
Body action / Joint action	Draws scapula upwards and forwards / Elevates shoulder	Cervical vertebrae; flexor laterally extends shoulder joint / Sideways movement of head and neck, when acts singly (see 'forearm')	Rotates head to opposite side of flexion / Extends neck and flexes to side of contraction	Rotate atlas / Extend head and neck, flex head and neck laterally if acting singly
Origin	Occiput — dorsal midline of neck thoracic spine 2–7	Wing of atlas and mastoid process, temporal bone, nuchal crest	Last five cervical vertebrae articular processes	Transverse processes of 1st two thoracic vertebrae
Insertion	Scapular cartilage — medial surface on dorsal border	Humerus — deltoid tuberosity and fascia shoulder and arm	Cervical vertebra — spinous and articular processes	Mastoid process wing of atlas, tendon in common with splenius and brachiocephalicus
Nerve supply	6th and 7th cervical nerves, ventral branches	Spinal accessory nerve, cervical nerve, axillary nerve	Last six cervical nerves, dorsal branches	Last six cervical nerves, dorsal branches
Blood supply	Dorsal artery, deep cervical artery	Inferior cervical artery, carotid artery, vertebral artery	Vertebral artery	Vertebral artery and deep cervical artery
Development problems	Loss of activity in shoulders/forehand. Affects coordination; stiff/tight muscles cannot stretch	Gait not level in front: worse on turns and circles; not going forwards, choppy strides	Resistance in neck action, feels tight, poor contact with bit	Head unlevel; neck tight and stiff. One side difficult to flex and does not take contact. Head shaking, unsteady. Cannot extend head

Table 2.2 Shoulder extensors.

	Brachiocephalicus	Supraspinatus	Infraspinatus	Subscapularis
Location				
Joint action	Extensor	Extensor and support — acts as lateral ligament	Supports and stabilises acts as lateral ligament	Support; adducts humerus
Body action	Protracts fore limb, raises shoulder and pulls it forward	Advances the fore limb	Abducts forearm and rotates outwards	Adductor of fore limb; prevents limb moving outwards
Origin	Wing of atlas and mastoid process, nuchal crest	Scapula — cartilage and spine; supraspinous fossa	Scapula — infraspinous fossa and cartilage	Subscapular fossa, medial side
Insertion	Humerus — above deltoid tuberosity and distal crest, elongated line attachment	Humerus — lateral tuberosity	Humerus — caudal part of lateral tuberosity	Humerus — medial tuberosity
Nerve supply	Spinal accessory nerve and dorsal and ventral branches; axillary nerve, cervical nerve	Suprascapular nerve	Subscapular nerve	Subscapular nerve
Blood supply	Inferior cervical artery, carotid artery, vertebral artery	Suprascapular artery	Circumflex scapular artery	Subscapular artery
Development problems	Cause shoulder tightness or joint instability			

Table 2.3 Shoulder adductors and abductors.

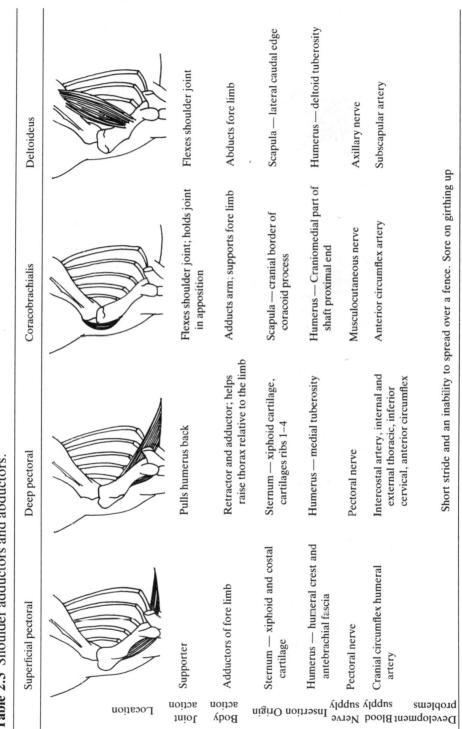

	Superficial pectoral	Deep pectoral	Coracobrachialis	Deltoideus
Location				
Joint action	Supporter	Pulls humerus back	Flexes shoulder joint; holds joint in apposition	Flexes shoulder joint
Body action	Adductors of fore limb	Retractor and adductor; helps raise thorax relative to the limb	Adducts arm; supports fore limb	Abducts fore limb
Insertion	Sternum — xiphoid and costal cartilage	Sternum — xiphoid cartilage, cartilages ribs 1–4	Scapula — cranial border of coracoid process	Scapula — lateral caudal edge
Origin	Humerus — humeral crest and antebrachial fascia	Humerus — medial tuberosity	Humerus — Craniomedial part of shaft proximal end	Humerus — deltoid tuberosity
Nerve supply	Pectoral nerve	Pectoral nerve	Musculocutaneous nerve	Axillary nerve
Blood supply	Cranial circumflex humeral artery	Intercostal artery, internal and external thoracic, inferior cervical, anterior circumflex	Anterior circumflex artery	Subscapular artery
Development problems		Short stride and an inability to spread over a fence. Sore on girthing up		

Table 2.4 Shoulder flexors.

	Latissimus dorsi	Seratus ventralis
Location	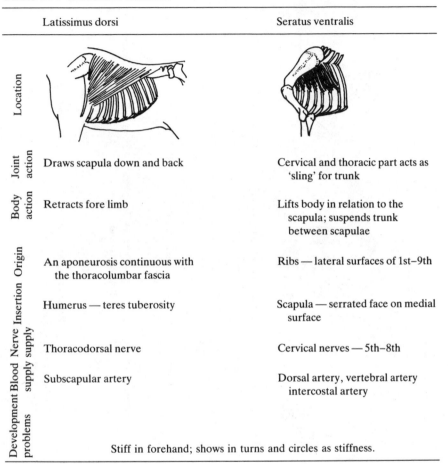	
Joint action	Draws scapula down and back	Cervical and thoracic part acts as 'sling' for trunk
Body action	Retracts fore limb	Lifts body in relation to the scapula; suspends trunk between scapulae
Origin	An aponeurosis continuous with the thoracolumbar fascia	Ribs — lateral surfaces of 1st–9th
Insertion	Humerus — teres tuberosity	Scapula — serrated face on medial surface
Nerve supply	Thoracodorsal nerve	Cervical nerves — 5th–8th
Blood supply	Subscapular artery	Dorsal artery, vertebral artery intercostal artery
Development problems	Stiff in forehand; shows in turns and circles as stiffness.	

Table 2.5 Back.

	Latissimus dorsi	Levatores costarum	Longissimus costarum
Location			
Joint action	Draws humerus up and back; supports dorsal part of thorax flexes shoulder joint	Rotation and lateral flexion of spine	Extends spine; depresses and retracts ribs; expiration
Body action	Retracts fore limb and draws trunk forwards when limb fixed	Draws ribs forwards for inspiration	Lateral flexion of trunk
Origin	Thoracic spines, withers and an aponeurosis continuous with the thoracolumbar fascia over caudal thorax	Transverse processes of thoracic vertebrae	Lumbar transverse processes last 15 ribs — anterior lateral surfaces lumbodorsal fascia
Insertion	Humerus — teres tubercle	Lateral surfaces and anterior borders of upper ends of ribs	Posterior borders of ribs; transverse process of the last cervical vertebrae
Nerve supply	Thoracodorsal nerve	Intercostal nerve	Thoracic nerve
Blood supply	Subscapular artery, intercostal artery, lumbar artery	Intercostal artery	Intercostal artery
Development problems	Cause sore, tight backs and a stiff wooden feel to the rider		

Table 2.6 Hamstrings, extensors.

	Biceps femoris	Semitendinosus	Semimembranosus	Gluteus medius
Location				
Joint action	Extends hip joint; flexes stifle joint; main belly flexes hock; anterior part extends stifle	Extends hip and hock and flexes stifle	Extends hip joint	Extends hip joint
Body action	Extends and abducts the hind limb and propulsion; rearing, kicking	Propulsion of trunk; rotates limb inwards; rearing	Adducts hind limb	Abducts limb strong hip extensor rearing, kicking, propulsion
Origin	Ischiatic spine, and tuber ischium and sacral vertebrae; sacroiliac ligaments	Tuber ischium — mid ventral area, and ilium — mid shaft	Tuber ischium — medial ventral border and sacrosciatic ligament	Ilium — gluteal surface and crest and aponeurosis of longissimus lumorum
Insertion	Femur — 3rd trochanter, patella and lateral ligament tibial crest, crural fascia to hock	Tibial crest and fascia part joins tarsal tendon of biceps femoris which attaches to tuber calcis	Femur — medial epicondyle; stifle — medial side	Femur — trochanter major
Nerve supply	Posterior gluteal nerve, sciatic nerve, and branches tibial and caudal, gluteal, peroneal nerves	Great sciatic nerve	Great sciatic nerve	Cranial and gluteal nerve
Blood supply	Gluteal artery and obturator branch; deep femoral artery; posterior femoral artery	Posterior gluteal artery; obturator artery; deep femoral artery; posterior femoral artery	Posterior gluteal artery; obturator artery; femoral artery	Gluteal, iliolumbar artery; lumbar artery; iliacofemoral artery
Development problems	Shortening of forward stride, resist lateral movements, discomfort in hind joints			

cation of the muscle. Rows two and three describe the muscle's action on the joints and body. Rows four and five indicate where the muscle begins and ends, and six and seven show the nerve and blood supply. Finally, row eight describes problems you may have if the muscle is not working as it should.

3
Profiling

We have considered the ideal equine athlete in terms of his conformation, movement and temperament. The next step is to consider how closely our own horse conforms to this ideal. To do this we need to build up a profile of our horse. The profile will consist of several parts:

- photographs
- past history and general description
- tables of specific measurements

The first thing to do is train your eye, so let's take a trip to the stable with this book in one hand and a pencil in the other so that we can establish a base to work from! The aim is to complete Table 3.1. It shows the kind of information which you may already have or can easily obtain, for example a detailed general description and history of your horse.

Photographs of the front, sides and rear of your horse form an essential part of all the assessments, and it is strongly recommended that you obtain some good quality colour pictures right from the start. Remember, however, that photographs do not reveal the whole truth and may on occasions be misleading. The adage 'The camera never lies' is not always true. These photographs and descriptions are the beginning of your horse's 'profile'.

Ideally a profile should start at birth or at purchase. However, we are going to start now. Go to your horse, look at him critically, and then complete Table 3.2 (initial section only) which shows your personal observations of his conformation. As you progress through this book, you will be advised when to complete the next assessment in this table; you should do this without reference to your initial observations, and then make comparisons. If you don't cheat, you may find that your eye has become more professional and the latest assessment a little more realistic. After all, we all think our geese are swans!

Assessing and monitoring your horse provides a profile of his performance potential which is the basis of his future development plans. Correctly carried out the profile will ultimately increase your horse's value and performance.

Table 3.1 General description.

Name of horse:	William of Orange II
Age	6
Height	16.0 hh
Colour	Bay
Breeding	Registered Dutch Warmblood
Stage of Training	Novice BHS Events (2 points), elementary dressage, Newcomers
Previous injuries	None
Weight, condition	550 kg, good.
Temperament	Good
Past history	Imported as 5-year-old. With present owner 18 months
Other notes	

Assessments can help in the choosing of your new horse, and influence his subsequent management and riding programme. Continuous assessment should act as an early warning system and show whether you are carrying out the correct development programme. It is now up to you; the horse's future is in your hands, of course with the guidance which this book can give.

There are many areas of assessment but we can list them under a few main headings such as:

- skeletal measurement
- the developed shape of the horse (chapter 4)
- the feet
- movement and action
- mouth assessment
- temperament
- condition

When all the information you have gathered and recorded in the tables is finally put together, it will produce a comprehensive profile of your horse. Think of the profile as your horse condensed on to paper. It contains his history, description, measurements and assessments,

Table 3.2 Observation of conformation.

Name of horse:	William of Orange II
Date	30 August 1990
Head	Attractive; in proportion to body
Neck	Good length and top line. Well set on to head and shoulder
Shoulder/wither	Slightly upright shoulder, wither not very well defined
Fore leg	Short cannon, $8\frac{3}{4}$ in (20 cm) of bone. Pasterns rather upright. Round joints
Girth/barrel	Slightly lacking depth; strong behind saddle
Hindquarter	Falls away behind croup but tail well set on
Hind leg	Good second thigh, hocks fleshy. Wind galls
Feet	Lacking heel all round. Off hind spread to outside

personal foibles and idiosyncrasies and any other records and information that may prove useful. The profile will help the horse throughout his life, provided, of course, that it is regularly updated. It should, for example, prevent the same problems from arising again and again.

Before you go on to complete the tables, it may be a good plan to list the reasons why you have a horse. This is not as silly as it sounds: you should decide exactly what you expect of him, and how far you wish him to progress in your original choice of activity. The profile you build up should soon be able to help you decide whether your particular horse is capable of development to a high standard of proficiency in that activity, or whether his development potential is better suited to a different discipline. This does not mean a horse cannot have his development and training programme tailored to suit a specific discipline, but the mechanical structure of a particular horse may impose certain limitations.

It may of course be that you keep him just to ride for relaxation and for his companionship. Even so, any time spent in development training will help to keep him sound, active and stress free, and will improve the rapport between horse and rider.

If you are inclined towards competition work, you must be prepared to spend a lot of time with your horse. If your time is limited, you may be able to place your horse in livery or find someone to help. What time you have should then be concentrated upon the development and training programme. The more sophisticated the facilities available to you, the easier it will be to carry out your work programmes, but no such sophistication can substitute for commitment and understanding.

Perhaps you are a serious student of the horse and would not wish to limit your experience to just one animal and one discipline. Discuss these matters with your instructor or trainer and then define your goals and ambitions clearly. Review these periodically because although, once the plans are made, one would not anticipate a need for frequent or major review, slight variations can be expected.

A lot has been written about conformation and the importance of good conformation in athletic performance. Because of the variety of disciplines we prefer to substitute 'relevant' in the place of 'good', as for each discipline there is a 'shape' more suited to the activity, producing less stress and strain.

Conformation consists of two fundamental aspects, skeletal conformation and developmental conformation. The skeleton is the framework of the horse, and apart from some bone remodelling it will not alter after maturity except through serious injury or neglect.

The development of the horse, its muscles, connective tissue and fat, will give it its shape or posture, and over- or under-development in different areas may give a picture to the observer which does not necessarily reflect what may be a perfect skeletal formation. On the other hand the horse may appear to have a perfect shape and yet have a framework that is slightly out of proportion. The reason the horse looks perfect is that a planned development programme has compensated for its slight imperfection. This is one of the reasons why show horses are frequently presented overweight.

The Skeleton

Now we are ready to take detailed measurements of the horse's bones, bearing in mind that soft tissue conceals some of the frame. This is where the fun starts!

Table 3.3 shows comparative measurements of three horses, Henry, Xanadu and Charlie (Figs. 3.1, 3.2 and 3.3). Remember you are measuring bone and the framework of the skeleton. Do not follow the contours of the body: go from point to point; use a stick to make right

Table 3.3 Comparison of three horses.

	Henry	Xanadu	Charlie	
Height	15 hh	16.2 hh	16.3 hh	
Age (years)	9	13	6	
Head A–B	24	20	24	Despite their different types all
Back C–D	25	20	26	three horses conforms to the
Depth E–F	27	21	29	standard quite well.
Stifle to hock M–K	23	21	24	Henry: short legs and deep girth.
Shoulder H–G	24	23	26	Xanadu: exceptional shoulder.
Elbow to fetlock I–J	23	20	26	Charlie: Slightly long in leg and
Hock to ground K–L	24	20	26	back.
Height G–L	62	51	67	Charlie: long and slightly croup
Length N–O	65	54	71	high. Height more than 2'2 the
Croup height P–L	62	52	68	standard.
				Xanadu: conforms closely to the
				ideal except for long shoulder.
				Henry: almost ideal.
Thickness of head Q–V	14	11	12	Charlie: Ideal.
				Xanadu: Ideal.
Attachment of head V–W	15	11	13	Henry: Thick.
Front of withers to bottom of neck X–Y	21	18	21'2	Charlie: Good hind quarter but short in neck.
Bottom of neck to throat Y–U	18	14	18	Xanadu: Excellent shoulder but short in neck.
Haunch to point of buttock D–O	20	18	23	Henry: rather large head.
Point of buttock to stifle O–M	20	17	23	
Other notes				

Note: These measurements are taken from Figs. 3.1, 3.2 and 3.3 and are therefore only comparative.

angles and measure in a straight line, and enter your results in Table 3.3.

Each part to be measured is clearly illustrated and explained in Fig. 3.4 and Figs. 3.7–3.9. Make sure your horse is on a flat surface, has equal weight on all four legs, and is standing as squarely as possible with his head in its normal position. Try to ensure that there are no distractions.

Once we have the individual measurements of your horse's skeletal frame, we will study and evaluate them. These measurements indicate the good points and the points which, with careful development work, can reduce stress and give support to the horse. Depending upon the

Fig. 3.1 Henry

Fig. 3.2 Xanadu

results of the evaluation we will be able to suggest areas that will need to be included in your final development programme.

At this stage it is important to remind you that we are concerned with the evaluation of the *whole* horse and not just imbalances which may have been revealed by any of the measurements so far. There may be other compensatory factors which are supporting these differences.

Fig. 3.3 Charlie

For example, if your horse's head is on the large side, this could affect his balance, but if he has a good strong neck, perhaps a little shorter than the average, this would adjust the balance. You must also keep firmly in mind when evaluating that, to perform well, the principles of biomechanics, which include balance and lever action, are related to the activity. For example, a racehorse's balance must be at its optimum when at full gallop, whereas with a dressage horse balance must be at its best in the slower movements.

The first set of measurements in Table 3.3 should be nearly equal in proportion. However, some variations for different activities can be expected.

The head (Fig. 3.4 A–B) is usually used as the 'standard'. If it is larger than the other measurements but the majority of the others are similar, use one of these others. Obviously the length of the head is to some extent related to its weight, which is a considerable proportion of its total body weight. It contains over 34 bones and 36 to 40 teeth, and it plays an important role in the balance of the horse.

The back measurement (Fig. 3.4 C–D) is taken from the posterior angle of the scapula to the haunch (known as the thoracic/lumbar areas). It should be the same as, or similar to, the 'standard' measurement. This measurement gives us some information about the weight the horse can carry and for how long, before he loses some athletic ability imposed by weight.

We know some horses can carry weight for long periods of time, and we know that it causes stress and impairs performance. This is an in-

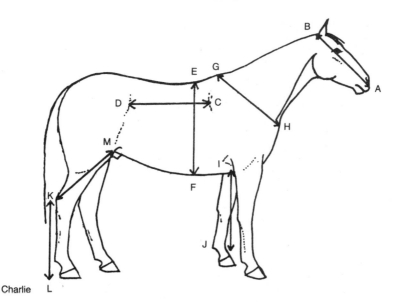

Fig. 3.4 A–B   The standard; C–D   posterior angle of the scapula to the haunch; E–F   depth of body from bottom of withers to just behind girth; M–K   lower fold of stifle to point of hock; H–G   shoulder; I–J   elbow to just above fetlock joint; K–L   point of hock to ground. These measurements should all be the same or equal.

creasingly important factor with growing demands in the performance activities. In the horse's thoracic spine, bending and rotation are minimal in front of the ninth thoracic vertebrae and maximal around the eleventh and twelfth thoracic vertebrae. Remember that this is just beneath the saddle on which you sit, making this area very vulnerable. Stress to the joints in the back can often manifest itself as stresses in the limbs and the feet because of the compensation the horse has had to make to relieve stress in the back. Can you remember having a backache and finding a position or posture that was comfortable? On looking in the mirror you were lopsided, the weight of your whole body centred down one side: think about the strain that is thus imposed on one of your legs.

If C–D is longer than the 'standard', the back is weak from the weight-carrying point of view. Stress will be put on to the lumbar region and the lumbosacral joint (Fig. 3.5). Even though the lumbosacral joint has limited action, the ability of the horse to move well is dependent on this joint's full function. The lumbosacral joint is situated between the last loin vertebrae and the rump. Its position should be as far forward as possible in front of the sacroiliac prominences. However, we must not get confused with the sacroiliac joint (Fig. 3.6). The lumbosacral joint is part of the spine. It articulates

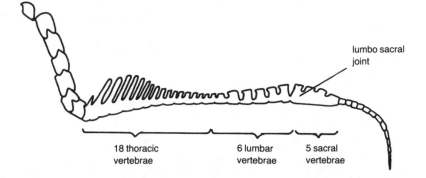

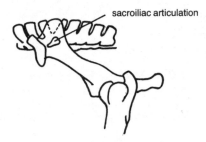

Fig. 3.5 Lumbosacral joint. This is where the lumbar and sacral vertebrae meet.

Fig. 3.6 Sacroiliac joint. The pelvis is attached to the sacrum via the sacroiliac joints.

from the last lumbar vertebrae with the sacrum, and acts to transmit the impulsion generated by the hindquarters to the forehand. Its flexibility, although limited, allows the pelvis and the hindquarters to rotate forwards beneath the horse's body when moving at the gallop and at the canter, when jumping, and when engaging the hindquarters to raise the back. This rotation takes place mainly when both hind limbs move forwards (protract). At the walk and trot both rear legs are moving in opposite directions, and because the lumbosacral joint is incapable of sideways flexion some of this movement is taken up by the sacroiliac joints. This area can be strengthened and supported with the correct muscle development. Any excessive lumbar length gives added lever action to the joint, increasing stress.

The horse's skeletal system was not designed to carry compressive weight from above but to carry in suspension a huge gut and for the mare to carry her foal. Carrying the rider's weight increases the demands on the horse's back, and these demands on the joints of the spine sometimes produce more stress than can be coped with. Extra length will increase the stress even further, so we look for a short, strong lumbar region placed as far forwards as possible, giving a long croup which can accommodate a good muscle mass.

The next measurement is the depth of the body from the bottom of the withers where the back is flatter, in a straight line to the bottom edge of the abdomen just behind the girth, labelled E to F (Fig. 3.4). This too should approximate to the standard measurement. The more weight the horse is asked to carry for any length of time, the greater this measurement should be. Remember that the heart and lungs are housed in this area and there must be adequate room for these organs. The importance of the relationship of the last two measurements to each other is obvious: if the horse is long in the back, the greater the stress on the lumbosacral joint; if, however, it is supported by a deep girth, the stress will be reduced to some extent. On the other hand, if the horse has a long back and little depth, much more development work will be required.

The measurement of the stifle to the hock (M to K, Fig. 3.4) should approximate to the standard, again with variations for different activities. Any excess length would indicate good speed potential, and lesser measurements would point towards greater ability in the slower movements requiring more elevation.

The measurement of the shoulder or scapula (H to G, Fig. 3.4) should be as long as the standard; if too long, it will give a low set to the upper arm (the humerus), thus creating a sharper angle. If too short, the room for the length of the important muscles will be reduced.

The area from the elbow to just above the fetlock joint (I to J, Fig. 3.4) needs to be in proportion to the standard. If the recordings indicate too much or insufficient length, problems may arise.

The last measurement in this section is from the hocks to the ground (K to L, Fig. 3.4). If longer or shorter than the standard, there is some weakness which must either be given support or observed for compensatory factors when we come to analyse the whole horse.

The next two measurements, height (G to L) and length (N to O, Fig. 3.7) will reveal some interesting points. These measurements should be equal to two-and-a-half times the standard, and they should be equal to each other. This is more important in the horse that has to carry weight for any length of time and is less so for a horse carrying lighter weights for short times only. It will in all probability be better for the horse to be longer than it is high, but this will depend on other aspects of his conformation. Compare the hunter, which has to carry a substantial weight for the better part of a day that includes jumping and galloping, with a racehorse, which may carry weight for only a few minutes in a race. A hunter with an excess of length over height will lose athletic ability and will become fatigued and stressed more quickly.

If, on the other hand, the horse is higher than he is long, the devel-

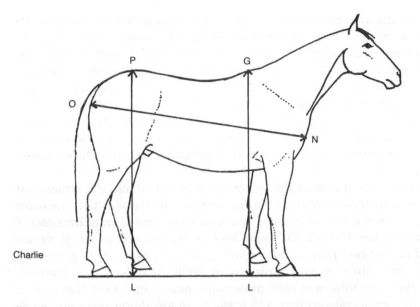

Charlie

Fig. 3.7 G–L   Height of withers; N–O   length; P–L   height of croup.

opment necessary to produce the more collected frame will shorten his base of support further. If he is made to do this, his balance will be compromised and then his gaits will be rushed. We should develop his self-carriage only enough to enable him to use himself effectively, and care will be needed to keep his back as supple as possible and the lumbosacral joint as stress-free as possible.

Some degree of imbalance in the skeletal frame can be compensated for if it is taken into consideration when planning the horse's overall development programme. If you know that the horse's conformation may produce strain on a joint, you can give the area more support and care. If the total body length of the horse (N to O) is greater than two-and-a-half times the 'standard' measurement, we must investigate to locate the section in which the excess length occurs. If the C to D (Fig. 3.4) measurement is approximate to the standard measurement, then either N to C or D to O or both must be greater in distance. On the other hand, if C to D is greater than the standard, then the distance between N and C, and D and O, or both, must be shorter. Should the back measurement of C to D be shorter than the standard, the horse will in all probability have a less supple back.

We will now consider the height of the croup off the ground (P to L, Fig. 3.7). If the horse is higher at the croup than at the withers, he will give a downhill ride, pushing more weight on to the forehand. The greater the difference the more this is accentuated, making it more difficult to lighten his forehand which is necessary for gymnastic work.

The saddle will need to be fitted even more carefully because of the increase in the forward momentum of the rider which would otherwise compromise the shoulder action. The increased weight on the fore-hand will cause increased stress and strain on the front limbs and feet. Provided that the horse is not too croup high, we can develop him to elevate his forehand and to lower his croup, making his sling system (the attachment of the forehand to the body) as effective as possible thus reducing the effects of his imbalance. Again this is less of a problem with a racehorse moving at speed than with a horse doing gymnastic work.

The measurements of the thickness of the head and the attachment of the head (Q–U–W, Fig. 3.8) should be half the standard measure-ment. This is very important if you wish to do any form of dressage: if he cannot flex his poll and relax his bottom jaw comfortably, he will resist collection. This resistance will develop muscle which is bulging, short and tight with no suppleness or ability to stretch and contract. This type of problem is very common in horses that have been forced into an unnatural position which their conformation does not easily permit. It causes unnecessary fatigue as a result of a too demanding schooling programme. These bulges of muscle can be quite painful to the touch and can be the cause of 'head shyness'. When human beings have tight, stressed neck muscles, they may suffer from headaches. The

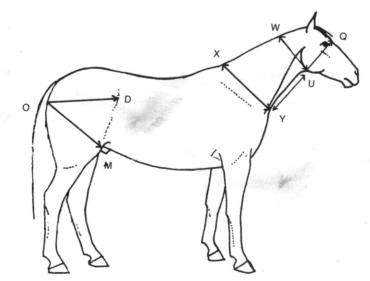

Charlie

Fig. 3.8 Q–U   Thickness of the head; U–W   attachment of the head; X–Y   In front of withers to bottom of neck; Y–U   bottom of neck to throat; D–O   haunch to point of buttock; O–M   point of buttock to stifle. These measurements should all be the same.

same may well happen in horses, and certainly, when this problem has been overcome, the relief can be seen from the facial expression.

The measurements from in front of the withers, X, to the bottom of the neck, Y, and from Y to the throat, U (Fig. 3.8) should be the same and are always shorter than the standard. These measurements should be identical to those in the hindquarters, D to O and O to M. The main point to be made is that they are in proportion to each other so that the action is balanced.

The position of the neck setting to the body is an important consideration. A neck which is in a horizontal position is better suited to speed than to the elevation required of a horse doing dressage work.

If the neck length in relation to the height of the horse is short, this will have an effect upon the balance of the horse. More importantly, however, if the horse is short in the neck and he finds that he must compensate in posture to graze, the effects of this altered posture will influence his development. For example, he may have to open his legs wide to graze, and this can cause uneven wear on his feet. If the feet are out of balance, this will create more problems, which we will discuss when we come to look at the foot measurements.

The next measurements are of the angle formed between the scapula and the horizontal, the angle formed between the humerus and the horizontal and the total angle formed by these two bones (Fig. 3.9). Their slope, length and angulation will influence the action of the

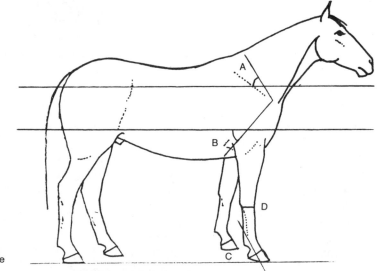

Fig. 3.9 A, Angle between scapula and horizontal. B, Angle between humerus and horizontal. Total angle should measure 110°. C, Pastern/fetlock/foot angle should be same as scapula angle. D, Bone measurement.

forehand and the position of the forehand's attachment to the body. Different angles of slope of the scapula and the humerus are called for according to the type of discipline the horse is asked to carry out, but the total angle should be about 110°.

The pastern/fetlock/foot angle is considered to be at the best mechanical advantage if it is the same as the scapula angle. Equally as important is that the fetlock/pastern angle be the same as the foot angle, and that the angle is the same at the toe and at the heel.

The next important measurement is the amount of 'bone' that the horse has (Fig. 3.9). To measure your horse's 'bone' means to see how much bone a horse possesses in the limb. This is taken using a tape measure around the horse's leg, just below the knee.

You will have recorded the weight of your horse in Table 3.1. Now that you have the 'bone' measurements you can calculate whether your horse has enough bone for his weight. The horse has very slender limbs which carry a heavy body, and this 'bone' measurement should relate to his total weight. As a general rule, 7 in of bone for each 1000 lb (18 cm per 460 kg) of body weight is acceptable. Some experts would question this as being low, and the authors would also prefer the horse to have more. However, it is a good guide for easy reference. Thus a 16.0 hh riding horse carrying a saddle and rider needs at least 8.5 in (22 cm) of bone.

Completing diagrams of the bone alignment of the limbs of your horse can be fun to do. If you have tried this in the past and had problems, you will find that the best way is to fasten a weight on to the end of a piece of string. With the horse standing as squarely as possible, position the string to hang down the middle of the leg (Fig. 1.2). Record the points of alignment by making a series of chalk dots on the horse's limbs where the limb makes contact down the length of the string. Unless the horse's leg is perfectly straight, you will find that the string does not make contact all the way down. It is important that, when transferring these dots to the diagram, the areas of non-alignment are accurately recorded. If necessary we may be able to improve and support the horse over a period of time and prevent unnecessary lameness. One of the authors recalls being told many years ago as a student that every horse she owned, cared for, trained or rode should be the better for it. What a wonderful philosophy to have when you are dealing with horses.

Finally, record the position of your horse's lumbosacral joint (Fig. 3.5). This will be of use later in the book. Table 3.3 shows a comparison of three horses in terms of their skeletal measurements.

If you find other areas of conformation that need special consideration, you can design your own forms on which to record the information which should subsequently be added to your horse's profile.

With this 'identikit' of your horse's biomechanical makeup we can now 'put the whole horse together'. The best way to do this is to use Fig. 3.10 and draw in your measurements using different colours for the different sections. If your horse's measurements are less than the 'standard', use dashes; if more, then indicate this by drawing an extra thick black line.

We can now see whether or not any areas which are not perfect can be adequately compensated for by drawing upon the good points. Perhaps by giving your horse support from some form of specialised development work we will be able to avoid the stress caused by any imperfections.

How will the horse's skeletal measurements affect his work?

- If your horse is lacking in mass or length in the hindquarters, he will not be able to provide adequate power for impulsion, propulsion or sustained activity. However, the placement of the bones in relation to the rest of the body will have some influence on the action of the joints and can provide compensation for some of these unequal proportions.

Fig. 3.10 For measurements of the whole horse.

- One example which will cause difficulty is a horse of equal proportions apart from having an excessively 'good' shoulder measurement (G to H). His action in front will be so good that the hindquarters will be dragged along causing stiffness and discomfort which will eventually sour him. If the trainer can see that the horse needs to be developed to balance the effects of his 'good' shoulder, he can avoid the problem of stress being imposed upon the rest of the body.

- If the head (A to B) is out of proportion to the rest of the standard measurements, this can be compensated for if the horse has a strong, short neck. This strong, short neck may not be conducive to speed, but it will help to compensate for the extra weight from the heavy head at the slower paces. The placement or set of the head and neck on the body will have an influence on the whole horse and may compensate for proportional imbalances. It can determine how the horse will carry himself and therefore how or which way he can perform best.

- The horizontal neck placement may have an advantage for speed but it will be hard to develop the base of the neck for the elevation needed for collecting the horse for dressage movements. A more vertical set with a firm base will be easier to develop.

- If the horse has a heavy head and a long, thin, low-set neck, this will place a lot of weight on the forehand. He will need a talented trainer to readjust his balance to perform well. This would of course depend on the natural ability the horse displayed as to whether he would be worth spending time on in training, and also whether the horse could stand the physical and mental strain of that development work.

- Before we leave the neck it is worth thinking about the position of the neck vertebrae and their shape. These vertebrae can determine problems such as 'ewe', 'swan' and 'upside' neck. They should form two, slightly sloping, even curves to give the best advantage to the horse. However, the above problems may not arise from the bone shape or placement; they may be caused by incorrect posture or incorrect development, as will become clear later.

- If your 'identikit' shows that the length of the stifle to hock (M to K) is much greater than the standard, as you may see in some steeplechase type horses, this may well indicate that your horse's potential is more towards galloping and jumping over fences at speed. Assessment of the walk and trot may show the hind limbs overtracking the front limbs so much as to make the gait unlevel. Although excessively long, out-of-proportion hind limbs allow a steeplechaser to do his job well, they can produce stress on other parts of the body because of these unequal proportions. This long element of the limbs, although good for extension at speed, is very difficult to flex and engage at the slower speeds.

Many people try to make into a dressage horse a horse more suited by his build for steeplechasing. Even with careful development, horses of this type will only be capable of a certain level of dressage work, but can still give their riders a lot of fun and valuable experience. The physical and mental stress is usually too much for such a horse if he is expected to proceed to a higher level.

The Feet

Monitoring of foot measurements can tell us a great deal about what is gradually happening inside the foot over such a long period of time that we may not notice the changes. As with step and stride measurements it can be of great assistance to your vet and your farrier as an aid to indicate what is wrong if your horse goes lame.

The horse has evolved so that he is now standing on the equivalent of the tip of your middle finger. The horn of the hoof grows downwards from the coronet band, and growth is believed to be stimulated by contact with the ground. The compression inside the foot as it takes weight will increase the circulation to the foot, bringing nutrients essential for growth.

The feet should be in proportion to the body in size: the more the horse weighs the larger the feet. It is important to record your horse's weight on a regular basis to monitor changes in condition and calculate rations. You do not need a weigh bridge for this: just use a tape measure and work out the formula or invest in a special weigh tape; this will be accurate enough. Always remember to record and date your results. At first, photographs will help as a guide.

The areas of the feet that we will be monitoring are the *angles*, the *wall height*, the *sole size*, the *heels* and the *coronet band*, the *rate of growth* and *balance of growth*, and *shoe wear*. Remember that the shod foot wears differently from the unshod one. In the shod foot the horn is protected by the shoe; if the horn growth is unbalanced, the shoe protects and often exaggerates the imbalance whereas in the unshod foot the part that is growing more quickly is worn away as there is nothing to protect it. If the horse's action is such that one side of the foot hits the ground first, then increased circulation through this area will encourage it to grow more quickly, compensating for the extra wear.

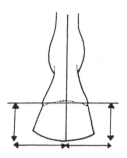

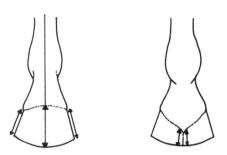

Fig. 3.11 Correct foot shape: a vertical axis through the centre of the cannon bisects the foot, i.e. there are two equal halves. A line running across the top of the coronary band is horizontal, i.e. the same distance from the ground on both sides of the hoof.

Fig. 3.12 Find a line running down the centre of the fetlock through the centre of the foot. Measure from the coronary band in five places: front, two sides and both heels.

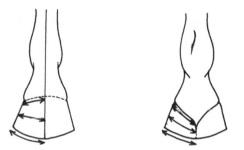

Fig. 3.13 Measure the coronary band circumference from heel to heel, checking that the measurements heel to heel and toe to heel are equal. Measure the circumference of the hoof halfway down the wall and at the bearing surface of the wall, again checking that the inside and outside of the hoof are equal.

Hoof Wall Measurement

The measurements of the hoof wall (Figs 3.11, 3.12 and 3.13) are taken around and from the coronet band in five places, not from the ground.

Hoof Angles

The hoof angles are taken from the heel, the middle of the foot and the toe (Fig. 3.14).

Hoof/Pastern Angle (Fig. 3.14)

Do the same measurements but include the pastern to the fetlock joint. This will show you any deviations between the foot and the pastern. It

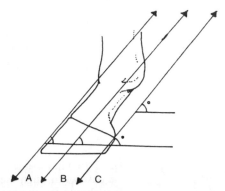

Fig. 3.14 Correct hoof–pastern angle. Lines A, B and C should be parallel so that the angles between the pedal, long pastern and short pastern bones are not broken. The heel should follow this line and not be collapsed. A correct hoof–pastern angle will indicate that the bones will carry the weight of the horse and rider in a balanced way. Measure A, B and C on your horse and record the measurements. Over a period of time, with the help of your farrier, you may be able to improve the shape of your horse's feet and reduce the stress caused by unbalanced weight distribution. Record before shoeing, trimming and afterwards, and date your findings. Depending on the horse's own conformation and type, and especially the angles formed by the shoulder and hip joints, a good range is between 45° and 55° to the horizontal.

is more important to have a continuous angle of foot and pastern than have the so-called ideal angle of 45° to 50° to the horizontal. The best way to do this is to use a protractor, a ruler and a piece of stick. Place the ruler along the heel so that it follows the angle the heel makes to the ground. Then use the protractor to measure the degree of angulation to the horizontal, marked C on Fig. 3.14. Repeat this, laying the ruler along the line made by the pedal bone, short pastern and long pastern (B), and finally measure the angulation of the front of the hoof to the horizontal (A). These three angles should be the same. Frequently horses have long toes and collapsed heels, placing strain on the flexor tendons during work.

The Sole of the Foot (Figs 3.15 and 3.16)

The sole of the foot can be measured by drawing a box around the horse's foot (Fig. 3.15). You can then compare the size of both front feet and both hind feet: they should fit in the same box. The size and shape of the box can also be used to look for changes in the foot which may indicate circulatory or movement problems.

The second way to examine the sole of the foot is to take a line which runs through the centre of the heel, the point of the frog and the centre of the toe (Fig. 3.16). This line should bisect the foot, in other words

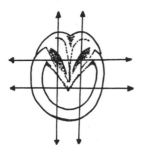

Fig. 3.15 Measurement of sole shape.

Fig. 3.16 Find a line from the back of the pastern through the heel to the toe. This should cut the foot into two equal halves. Measure the distance from this centre line to the wall at the heel, middle and towards the toe. The measurements of one half of the foot should be equal to those of the other half.

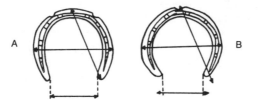

Fig. 3.17 (A) Correct shoe shape. The distance across the widest part of the shoe is equal to the distance from the centre toe to the heel; there are two clips allowing the shoe to be set further back on the foot, and the shoe is kept wide at the heel. (B) Incorrect shoe shape. The distance across the widest part of the shoe is greater than the distance from centre toe to heel. Shoe too narrow at heel.

the measurements from this line to either side of the foot at heel, mid point and toe should be the same.

The way to use these measurements is to recognise a good hoof–pastern angulation in proportion to the whole horse, and to work towards improving his angulation and hoof shape by regular trimming, reshoeing (Fig. 3.17) or corrective treatment. Monitor your horse as regularly as you can, remembering to date your monitorings, and compare your findings to see the progress. When changes take place in the foot for other reasons, you will be able to act as soon as you see a difference and to take the appropriate action far sooner.

Movement and Action

It is important to monitor the paths and directions in which the feet go, the flight and degree of elevation of each limb, the foot placements and lastly the position of the limbs at the walk (Fig. 2.19). Remember: at

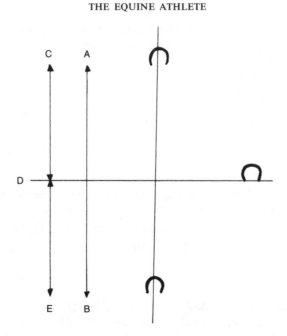

Fig. 3.18 Step and stride measurements. For each foot measure the total length of the stride (A–B) and each half of the stride, in front of the opposite foot (C–D) and behind the opposite foot (D–E).

Your findings

(1) The posterior part of the stride may be shorter, therefore the anterior part is longer.
(2) The anterior part of the stride may be shorter, therefore the posterior part is longer. However, the total length of the stride of each limb may be the same.
(3) The stride length of one limb may be different so the horse cannot move in a straight line.
(4) The main point of all this effort is to measure in order to provide a basis for monitoring your horse's development and to provide an early warning system for problems that may be developing.
(5) If your horse suddenly shows a difference in step length, beware and act now to avoid problems in the future.

this stage we are looking at the fine tuning over eight walk strides. Lameness would be assessed at the trot. The next thing is to measure what can be called step and stride, using the veterinary interpretation. Although the format of Fig. 3.18 looks complicated, given a few minutes study its use will become clear.

Ideally you will need a straight sand track 20 m long and 1 m wide, or an indoor or outdoor school with a sand surface, to get the best impressions. When it comes to raking and rolling the sand, it is easier if you can enlist the help of a few friends.

If you can imagine a giant pair of dividers or a sergeant-major's pacing stick, then you will know the kind of instrument you must make, beg, borrow or buy to take these measurements rather than using a tape measure.

The Path and Placement of the Feet

These should be measured:

(a) on the straight;
(b) on a left circle;
(c) on a right circle (use same size of circle);
(d) in the rein back. Look for direction, equal imprint and weight on his feet and on the individual foot, i.e. toe in, toe out. Make sure he is making two tracks off side and near side and that the front and back are on the correct track.

Flight and Action

Observe the flight and action of the horse's limbs as he moves. Look for the hocks extending and flexing equally. The knees should also be moved in the same way. The hips and the top of the hindquarters should move equally and make equal triangles with the limbs. The head and neck should move in a level fashion, not dropping more on one diagonal than on another in trot. Look for the legs swinging out-wards (paddling) or inwards (plaiting) during movement.

You must also time and count the number of strides taken over the 20 m track. Ideally you should do this at the walk and trot, ridden and unridden, and look at the results. 'Rein back' steps should be recorded also.

You may find this hard to do at first, so it is worth practising as again the results are only as good as the person doing the assessment. Of course these results can show up rider problems as well, so it may be better if your trainer also rides the horse through the track and you compare the results.

The next stage is somewhat easier. Take your horse on to a hard road and listen to the sound his feet make when moving actively, first on a loose rein, secondly on the bit, and again both at the walk and trot. If you wish to go even further, find a hill and carry out the same procedure both up and down. You may find that a tape recorder is of very great benefit for this part of the assessment. Do not forget to state on the tape exactly what particular function you are doing.

Mouth Assessment

Mouth assessment is an essential part of your horse's profile and can give you much information about two main areas, general good health and comfort; and the type of bits to be recommended. Some horses go better with different bits for different activities. Others get confused by changes of bits and work better if restricted to one type. Separate bits may be needed for different objectives and perhaps at certain times in the learning phase.

The mouth is a very sensitive area, concerned with the collection of information about taste and texture which is then passed to the brain. A more common horse with a more fleshy mouth is likely to be less sensitive in this area than a thoroughbred type. The degree of sensitivity of the tissues of the mouth varies as with humans, and a great deal of information can be gained from frequent assessment.

Because this region is so sensitive, it is very important that the mouth is assessed regularly and carefully. Dental health and hygiene are areas of stable management that are surprisingly neglected, and very often serious health and condition problems arise that stem from something as simple as an overlooked wolf tooth. Good routine care of the horse's mouth and teeth makes economic sense. The horse may not be showing clinical signs of tooth problems such as quidding, but slight mouth discomfort leads to poor performance, adds stress and can affect the horse's temperament and long-term health.

Horses manage to survive in the wild without tooth problems so why is the domesticated horse so susceptible? First we must look at the anatomy of the horse's head. The top jaw is wider than the bottom jaw, and the more quality the horse has the more pronounced this overlap. Consequently, when the horse is chewing, not all of the surface of the top molars grinds over the bottom molars. This will mean that as horse's teeth grow continuously the outside of the top molars and the inside of the bottom molars are not worn away, leaving sharp edges which can cause a great deal of pain to the horse (Fig. 3.19).

Secondly the domesticated horse's diet is quite different from that of the wild horse. The horse is designed to eat grass, which contains silica, a very hard abrasive substance. This, combined with the fact that the wild horse would be eating for 10 to 12 hours a day, wears the teeth

Fig. 3.19 The top jaw is wider than the bottom jaw leading to sharp edges on the molar teeth.

down effectively. The stabled horse may be receiving half his daily ration as soft and appetising foods such as cubes, oats and bran which he can eat very quickly and easily, not needing to use the full grinding surfaces of the molars. In the wild, horses naturally eat soil as they graze close to the roots of the grass and they may also have to resort to chewing bark and branches, all of which will help rasp the teeth naturally and remove the caps from milk teeth. Watch for your horse chewing the fence or licking the soil: he may need his teeth checking. Dogs and cats have the same instinct to keep their teeth not just sharp but healthy. Provided the dog gets his bone or the equivalent, he does not do a bad job!

How can you tell if your horse needs his teeth looking at? Watch your horse eat; watch him graze. Does he look happy when he is eating? Is there any anxiety? Watch his expression. Does he drop food out of his mouth? Is he refusing to eat? If you think he is different from other horses, or if you think anything about his eating is unusual or abnormal, note it down. It may or may not be important. It may confirm something else which you will find later on.

Before looking into the horse's mouth in detail, look at the head as a whole (Figs 3.20 and 3.21). The first thing to assess and record is the head from in front of the horse: notice whether the tips and the roots of the ears are level. Gently feel both ears separately to see whether there is any tenderness or objection to their being handled. Do they move freely? Do both eyes look level, and are they the same size? Are there any strange lumps or bumps on the face? Put your hands on each side of the face, and gradually move your hands down from just below the eyes to the side of the mouth. Can you feel any heat or notice any unusual protrusions from either side of the jaw? If your horse reacts at

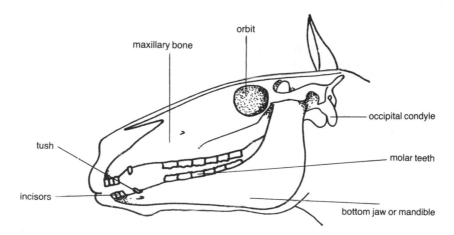

Fig. 3.20 The horse's skull.

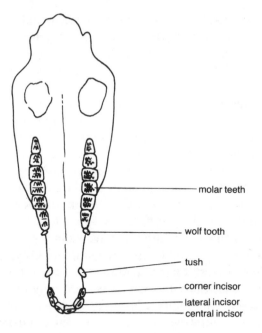

molar teeth

wolf tooth

tush

corner incisor

lateral incisor

central incisor

Fig. 3.21 Top jaw.

any time during this examination, note down which area causes discomfort as this may indicate tooth pain. Are the nostrils in line with each other? Are they the same size? Feel under the jaw: are there any painful lumps coming from the teeth? In some young horses the teeth in the jawbone are very crowded because the jawbone is still not fully grown. This can cause the lower jaw to feel lumpy and sometimes cause pain even if only slight pressure is applied. A noseband can cause irritation, and a breaking cavesson that has no padding under the jaw strap can also cause discomfort — especially if a lunge line is being used. This can be sufficient to influence the posture of the horse. He will protect his jaw by holding it stiff and his head high; the effects of this transmit through the back, and the posture and the natural gaits will be lost.

Check the bottom jaw for levelness as sometimes the mandibular joints are not balanced or have been knocked, and have healed in such a way that the growth of the teeth has been adversely affected. The bottom jawbone pivots on a part of the temporal bone just in front of the ear. The jaw houses the lower teeth and gives attachment to some of the muscles involved with chewing and swallowing. If the muscles are weak or have been damaged, the horse may have difficulty in getting the best from his food; feeding may be a uncomfortable process so the horse may only eat just enough to satisfy his hunger.

Look at the chin groove. Sometimes there is scar tissue which may have lost its sensitivity, or there may be a scarred lump which presses on to the bone. Check the lips for levelness and, more importantly, check the size of the lips in relation to the head and teeth.

Note how the horse's breath smells to you so that you can recognise future changes. You can quickly get into a routine of checking each time you put on the bridle. Changes in the smell may be caused by variations in the feed, but may also be a warning of something more serious.

Now inspect the corners of the horse's lips. They could be classified under one of the following headings: thin, padded, turned out, turned in, thick or thin. Note the amount of room between the corners of the mouth and the teeth. Record any scar tissue, cuts, etc.

Now we come to the part where you must look into the horse's mouth. This is something you should do on a regular basis. Initially this can be difficult if the horse has had some previous bad experience when having treatment or if he has been roughly handled because he had not been trained to open his mouth. If the horse has had his mouth opened regularly and gently, allowing you to inspect it, and he experiences no pain, he will cooperate when he needs treatment. The horse will usually stand still for treatment because of the trust he has developed in you following your care and patient training. He has no need to be apprehensive.

It is our job to make inspections as pleasant as possible. First we teach the horse to allow us to open and inspect his mouth. If we do this as a routine procedure with patience and tact, not forcing him but only asking for his cooperation, we can gradually ask more and more of him until eventually he allows us to open his mouth and move the tongue out to one side or the other.

Horses can learn to open their mouths for their teeth to be rasped. On the whole they do not like their teeth being rasped because, if they try to resist and in so doing move, the rasp may catch the gums and cause pain. If they stand still, there should be no need to hurt them.

The best way to begin is to stand in front of the horse. He should be wearing a head collar with an adjustable noseband so that there is no pressure on the nose when the jaws are open. With the right hand in the bars of the mouth, the left hand gently takes the tongue out to the left side, enabling the right-hand side to be inspected. With the thumb towards the roof of the mouth and the little finger towards the bottom bars, the tongue will be turned slightly up and therefore will not be pulled. By moving the tongue to the right side, the left side of the mouth and teeth will be visible. Do be very careful: horses' jaws are very powerful and their teeth are very sharp.

Practise this regularly until the horse will open his mouth on request.

This may not take more than a few days. A slim 'extra bright' torch is a great asset as it enables you to see a long way back in the mouth.

After each inspection the horse is rewarded by a small feed, or it is carried out just before the normal feed time. At each inspection demand a little more obedience from the horse. Be firm but gentle and remember to praise him for his cooperation: it is in the horse's nature to cooperate and he also likes to please so let him know when he has done well. When you feel confident in inspecting your horse's mouth, it will be possible for you to pull the inside cheeks away from the teeth to see if any are catching. You will then know whether the horse needs his teeth rasping. We would strongly recommend that you have your horse's teeth checked by a professional person (your vet or a trained equine dentist) twice a year. If your horse has had the training and routine inspection by you, he should not be too upset even when a gag has to be used.

Study Figs 3.20 and 3.21 before carrying out the assessment so that you have the objectives firmly in mind and can make sure that nothing is missed. The main point is to stick to a routine when carrying out your assessments.

Your first assessment will be the recording of the detailed conformation of your horse's mouth and how each part relates to the others. A small tongue is only small if it is small in relation to the jaw. A point to note is the size of the two jaws. Remember that the bottom jaw is naturally much narrower than the top and the teeth of the top jaw overlap the bottom jaw, and the horse grinds his food rather than chewing it: note how much the tables of the teeth overlap during this grinding. The ability of the tables of the teeth to be used in their entirety to grind is an important factor. The teeth are responsible for mechanical breakdown of the food which allows the enzymes that activate the digestive processes to penetrate the tough outer layers of grain and hay.

The tables should not be smooth but they must not have anything on the surfaces that will interfere with the grinding action. Areas for special attention are the outer edges of the top molars and the inner edges of the bottom ones.

Lacerations of the cheeks by sharp edges can become very sore and cause thickening of the cheeks with scar tissue. If the space between the teeth and the cheek tissue is already limited, any thickening of the tissue can make matters worse.

A horse one of the authors remembers had a large, sharp edge on a tooth which had made a neat hole in his cheek. When he was working he managed to place the sharp edge in this hole to prevent it from causing any further damage and pain. The result was that to maintain this position he had to fix his head so that the tooth did not move from the hole. It was believed from this unnatural position that there was a schooling problem. His general condition had deteriorated slightly, but he was still jumping well apart from being difficult to hold and control, and therefore his performance was affected. What a brave little horse! With all the specialist tack employed to stop him, he went on working in the only way he could, still managing to keep the tooth in the hole. After treatment and a little schooling in a special bridle called a scraw-brig (see Chapter 5 on tack), this horse regained confidence in his mouth. With some rehabilitation exercises he soon re-established his proper outline, lost because of his protective posture, and started winning his classes as his potential had always indicated he could.

The next things to look for are minor abnormalities and again to record your findings. One such example is *step mouth*, a condition in which the teeth are not even but make steps, which change the height of the tables. A *shear mouth* is an abnormality in which the teeth are shaped at an angle instead of having flat tables, the inner edges being shorter than the outer edges. Individual tooth problems also occur, such as breaks, splits, infections, malalignments causing hooking, the presence of wolf teeth, the retention of caps or crowns and food or foreign matter being caught in the tooth sockets which may cause abscesses to form.

A retained cap occurs when a milk tooth has not come away and has become fixed on to the top of the new tooth. As the new tooth grows to the level of the rest of the teeth, the cap will protrude, stopping the adjacent teeth contacting with those in the opposite jaw. This is more of a problem in young horses between three and five years of age that are out to grass. If the front incisors cannot bite the grass because they cannot meet, the horse will lose a lot of weight. Most horses that are allowed to graze will after a while manage to get rid of these caps, but some do not and they may hurt themselves trying.

Wolf teeth are vestigial molar teeth which appear in the spaces where the bit lies in the mouth and should be removed. They are usually found just in front of the top first molar but have been found anywhere on the bars. The main reason for removing these teeth is because they have very shallow roots and therefore can move within the jaw if anything interferes with them such as pressure from the bit.

If the jaws are out of alignment, resulting in a reduction of wear in either of the top two front molars and either of the bottom two rear molars, 'hooks' can develop. If you find a hook on the top first molar, there will most likely be one correspondingly on the very last molar of the bottom jaw. This kind of problem should be dealt with by your vet or equine dentist.

You may like to prepare a chart for your horse's teeth similar to the one your own dentist uses. When your equine dentist checks or gives treatment to your horse, get him to tell you the state of them and describe any treatment that he has carried out, and record this on your chart. Most professional people are quite pleased for you to get involved and enjoy coming to visit people who take an interest in their work.

Now we will look at the rest of the mouth including basic conformation. Note the size of the jaws in relation to the tongue. Does the tongue fit in the jaw neatly? Is it long, short, fat, thin, very strong or flabby and weak? Is the roof of the mouth high or low? Is there room for the bit? How long or short are the bars, especially between the tushes and the first molar tooth? Are the bars high, low, thick or very fine? How near are the first molars to the corner of the lips?

Measure the width of the mouth to determine the bit size. Do this by using a piece of dowelling with two rein stoppers. The dowelling is placed in the mouth with a stopper at each side. Close the stoppers on to the mouth making sure they fit comfortably. Remove the dowelling and measure the length including the stoppers. This will give you a proper starting size. Remember that some horses are still growing at four and five years, and the bit that fitted well at three years may not fit later.

If the horse has a dry mouth, either because he is making insufficient saliva or he is working with his mouth open, there are several possible causes: he may not have been schooled to accept the bit properly; he may be fitted with the wrong bit; or his tongue may be rather long causing him to work with his mouth open. It could also be a rider problem.

Whatever the cause, the matter must be corrected before the mouth becomes hard and insensitive. Do not blame the bit if the horse has not been 'mouthed' well. If the tongue is long so that the horse carries his mouth open, exposed to the air, it will make the mouth dry. A dry mouth is a hard mouth. If a heavy bit were to be used, it would flatten the tongue and would encourage some horses to drop the tongue even more. If the bit is placed higher in the mouth, i.e. towards the top jaw not towards the bottom molars, the horse will curl his tongue up so that he can keep contact with the bit and the tongue will no longer protrude. This can also help if the tongue is wide; the curling prevents the horse from accidentally biting his tongue. If the tongue is fat and the roof of the mouth low, even an average rubber bit would be too large to be comfortable.

For one reason or another, some horses get swellings just above the top incisors and at times this tissue can reach to the bottom of the incisors. This condition is called *lampas*, which is inflammation of the mucosa of the hard palate. Apart from being uncomfortable it can interfere with mucus secretion and can make grasping of food difficult;

also, food may be swallowed without correct mastication. Young horses have been known to swallow cubes and get them stuck in the throat, a potentially dangerous situation. Any swelling in the mouth feels very uncomfortable, and lampas can make the horse very wary about his mouth. A bad experience at this time from being handled or from a bit can stay in his memory. Lampas is more common in young, teething horses or in horses undergoing changes in their environment. It is quite surprising to see how many have this swelling in some form or other.

If the bit is too large or the mouth is very short, then the hinge on a jointed snaffle can irritate as well. If the jaw is small and the bars are short, care over the size and the height of the bit can be more important than the type. This is where a bit slightly narrower than one which your earlier measurement suggested, and placed higher than the usual recommended position, could suit the horse better.

If the first molars are positioned in the same plane as the corners of the lips, this can result in the corners being pinched on to the teeth. An 'eggbutt' snaffle will afford some protection, or 'biscuits' (rubber discs placed on each side of the mouthpiece) on each side of a loose ring snaffle could be tried.

Sometimes the tushes are placed quite high and the adjacent gum gets knocked and becomes inflamed. The tushes are the last teeth to become fully grown and can become very sore even in a five-year-old. If the bar between the first molar and the tush is narrow and inflamed, the horse will not be able to cope well with a double bridle. Before teaching your horse to accept a double bridle, it is advisable to check that the tushes are 'quiet'. The horse may perform with more comfort if the bit is placed higher in the mouth.

Factors such as the ability of the rider, the type of activity and the level of development the horse has reached will also bear upon your choice of bit.

With all this information plus your common sense and the advice given by your trainer you should be able to establish proper communications and rapport with your horse.

The tongue will tell a great deal about the horse's health. Is the tongue smooth, indented, cracked, injured or scarred? Is the colour good? Check the capillary return by putting pressure on the tongue, and note how much pressure you need to apply and how long it is before the colour returns. If the tongue goes dead with the minimum of pressure, think what the effects must be of continuous pressure from the bit exerted through your hands.

The roof of the mouth often gets knocked or bruised and can be very sensitive. The horse may adopt a posture in which he carries his head high and holds the bit in his teeth so that the roof of the mouth is protected. If you continue to ride him in this state, the protective compensation will cause strain and can set up worse problems such as aching in the back.

Young horses from two to perhaps five years of age are at times in some discomfort due to teething. The tissue in the mouth can become very inflamed, leading to a rise in the horse's temperature. This sometimes coincides with breaking times and when the horse is being educated in mouthing. Again, if the mouth is assessed regularly and we are aware of any painful periods, we can avoid education at these times. It can be the cause of bad habits or the horse resenting and resisting our demands. If the training programme cannot be stopped, readjust the work accordingly. Time given now may save hours of frustration later.

It is not possible in this book to mention all the permutations you may come across when examining different mouths, or to consider how these variations can relate to each other. But we hope that what you have read so far has made you think, and will enable you to understand the implications of all the differences you will come across.

4
Developing the equine athlete

Development

Your horse's profile is taking shape. You have gathered all your horse's history and general information, and you have assessed and collected measurements about his locomotion, his feet and his skeletal frame. These measurements give you an accurate blueprint for your profile, and will be valuable to you when you start the development programme. This programme must be tailor made so that the full athletic potential of your horse will be achieved; it must fit in with his general state of health, his temperament, his intelligence, his age and his mental and physical maturity.

Now we will look at what we can add about your horse's developed state and monitor his adaptation by some more measurements. The assessment of your horse's skeletal shape will have highlighted his shortcomings and imperfections. The better he has scored the fewer the problems. However, the main point is that you are now aware of them and they can be considered and included in your horse's personal development programme. These shortcomings along with the time that you have available and your degree of expertise will determine what level and range of performance he can be trained to achieve.

The range of performance possibilities may be more important to you than competing at a high level. Thus, for example, a family horse or pony may need to be versatile to fit in with the family's enjoyment. The demands in competitive horse activities are becoming increasingly professional with competitors needing to push themselves and their horses to higher levels as well as do a job, bring up a family and participate in many other responsibilities. Consequently such riders become frustrated because they cannot produce the results which need time to perfect, and the fun goes out of it. Perhaps working at different activities including all the family members will be greater fun and relaxation. An average, equally proportioned horse with a kind temperament and good basic development can be trained to drive in trail competitions or to do dressage, showjumping, western riding, hunter trials or any of the riding club activities and can even hunt during the winter. This may only be at lower levels in some activities, but what a great deal of fun you will all have.

As the perfect horse has not been born yet, you will have found a number of deviations from perfection in your measurements so far. Not to worry: if we had found perfection, we would not have the fun of watching improvements take place.

We may, however, have been surprised to find how well our horse did score, especially in his skeletal frame. If this is the case, why does his overall conformation look poor and his athletic performance not reach the standard which his good skeletal frame would suggest he is capable of? Providing your vet has found no health or soundness problems this must be because of either under-, imbalanced or incorrect development.

Your assessment of your horse's present development is the base from which you assess, measure, monitor and evaluate his improvement during his development programme. The assessment will include:

- a definition of development
- recognition of different levels of development
- criteria for different activities
- criteria governing successful schooling

Lastly we will look at different skeletal shapes, how horses compensate for these different shapes and the varying development needs. The aim is to train your eye to recognise any deviations from normal imbalances in a horse's development. As previously described, the two aspects which govern the conformation of the horse are the skeletal frame and its soft tissue covering; just because your horse has a well shaped skeleton does not necessarily mean that the 'covering', in other words the developed conformation, will be the best. On the other hand, the correctly developed horse may look very attractive and perform well but have an inferior skeletal frame. A horse that has been very carefully developed and supported to compensate for his skeletal defects can look and perform very well depending of course upon the degree of imperfection and the level of work expected.

Which horse suffers the most stress and strain: the horse with some imbalances in his skeletal proportions but developed so that he can support his limitations, or the horse with equal proportions that has not been properly developed for his work? Of course it depends upon the extent of the proportional imbalances, but in the authors' view the horse that has been incorrectly developed will always suffer the most. Before he can perform well consistently he will have to go back to basic development, and the strain of performing in an incorrect posture will have left its mark and the horse will take correspondingly longer to develop.

The development of the horse, whether correct or incorrect, will influence his performance capabilities, his chances of remaining sound and athletic, and his ability to perform consistently over a period of time.

Incorrect development will limit the horse's potential, and injury is waiting to happen. The horse will be unsafe to himself and to his rider because he cannot perform without discomfort and will soon give up trying and start evading work. The physical strain of working incorrectly will fatigue his muscles, and the consequent aches and soreness will prevent him from resting and recuperating. Eventually the cumulative effect will sour his temperament and he will say 'No more, thank you'.

Horses sometimes look undernourished and it may be thought that good food alone will put them right. However, they are frequently eating twice as much food as their well developed counterparts but are burning up more nervous and physical energy because their work is uncomfortable or painful. This does not mean that the underdeveloped horse should have his energy intake drastically reduced, but do remember his diet must be balanced in terms of quality, not just quantity. A lot of horses are fed too much energy and protein for the work they do which makes them hyperactive and difficult to ride.

The correct combination of exercise and feeding will help develop the muscles and ligaments to make the horse athletically fit. As with feeding, the work programme should be 'little and often'. Unfortunately one of the biggest constraints the horse owner experiences is time. Consequently we are inclined to cram the exercise programme into one session a day instead of a few shorter ones or longer slower ones.

The horse's development will reflect his work programme, management, correct rehabilitation after illness or injury, however slight, and care after exertion. Even the way he is transported can influence his development: work out how long a competition horse spends in transit! The horse stands with his weight braced and is continually adjusting his balance. Those muscles that resist the motion of the vehicle will develop in a tighter way than the others, especially after athletic exertion when some muscles will be tired. Travelling stress can be reduced with a little thought and planning, and each individual horse may be helped in different ways; the driver, position, mode of travel, ventilation, space available, floor covering, vibration and company can all affect how well the horse travels.

The surface on which you do most of your training will have an effect on the horse's development and should be as varied as possible depending upon his general fitness.

Assessment and Measurement of the Horse's Developed Shape

Make sure your horse is standing squarely on level ground with his weight spread equally on each limb. The head should be in a natural position with the nose perhaps level with the point of shoulder. The main aim is to use the same spot and the same stance each time you measure. Carry out the measurements and record and date the results twice to make sure you have them correct, or get someone to check them.

Top line (Fig. 4.1)

The top line is from poll to tail root. The horse should have his head and neck stretched with his nose level with his knees; again the main point is to have the same position each time you measure. Follow the contours of his neck, withers, back and croup to the root of the tail.

The top line of your horse will tell you a great deal about his development, any compensations in his carriage, wear and tear and past injuries in this area. The top line should be a smooth series of curves, each curve blending into the next with no sharp breaks, bulges, bony knobs, or sharp dips. These irregularities can be due to ligament dam-

Fig. 4.1 Top line; Under line; Neck measurements (in three places); Body (in two places).

age, hypertrophy or overdevelopment by resistance, pressure on the spinous processes, any stretched ligaments which give too much movement instead of holding the vertebrae together, and muscle imbalance. Fat can conceal skeletal problems but it cannot hide the effects of good or bad development. Your measurements will show you how balanced his development is, and the changes that take place between your measurements will be a guide to your future work programme.

Remember that all athletes including humans will have injuries, and however slight these will lead to weakness. If we know of the weak areas, we can support them. The top line measurement will change as the horse improves his posture. It is not necessarily the total length that will alter but the length of the component parts, so it is important to show these parts when you measure.

Other measurements are as follows:

Under line (Fig. 4.1)

The under line is from sternum to stifle level.

Neck (Fig. 4.1)

Measure the circumference of the neck in three places and record if the distance from windpipe to top line is the same on both sides.

Body (Fig. 4.1)

Measure the circumference of the body in two places, the bottom of the withers, and behind the last rib, including the total measurement and each side.

Breadth (Figs 4.2 and 4.3)

Measure from point of shoulder to point of shoulder, and point of hip to point of hip over the top of the body and round the back of the quarters.

Length (Fig. 4.4)

Measure the total length from point of shoulder to buttock each side, remembering to include the contours of the muscles, and from the croup to the top of the stifle and to the buttock each side.

Limbs

Measure each fore limb in three places: above the knee, total and front to back. Measure the hindquarters from the top fold of stifle to the

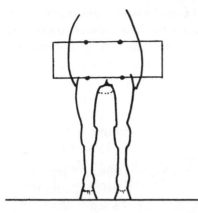

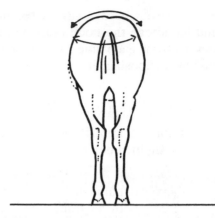

Fig. 4.2 Breadth of forehand. Draw a box on the front of your horse to correspond to the points of the shoulders and the points of the elbows. Ideally these points should align. If the elbows turn away from the body in relation to the point of shoulder, the whole limb may turn in. If the elbows are close to the body, the whole limb will turn out.

Fig. 4.3 Breadth of hindquarters.

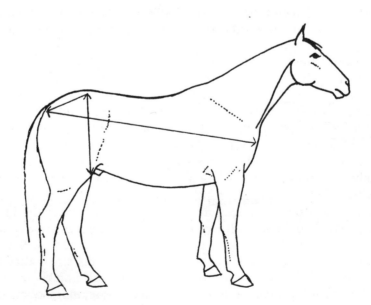

Fig. 4.4 Length.

opposite stifle, from stifle to the back of and inside each stifle. The hind leg above the hock must be measured in three places, total and back to front each side. You may wish to do other measurements of your own choosing.

Criteria Governing Successful Schooling

The important criteria governing successful schooling development and training include:

(1) *Calmness*. At each stage the horse must be *calm* and free from anxiety, pain, discomfort and confusion. He should cooperate freely with his trainer and accept the trainer's leadership.

(2) *Forwards movement*. The horse must go forwards with confidence and freedom of movement and with confined energy held in control.

(3) *Straightness*. The horse's body must move in a balanced posture and be as equally developed on both sides as his progress permits.

(4) *Steady progression*. One major part of the individual development programme is a steady progression depending on the horse's ability to respond without painful resistance. He must not be asked to do something that would subject his body to undue stress, and no demands must be made that will make him compensate in his posture or his movement patterns.

What is the difference between schooling and development? The schooling and the development of the horse usually go alongside each other. We can define the terms as follows. Schooling is the teaching of and learning by the horse of the skills he will need. Development is the change in body structures that allows the horse to adapt to his work. Development and schooling also have a mental element: as the horse's body adapts to his work, the work becomes easier and the horse gains confidence and enjoys his work. You know how tired and depressed you feel when your muscles will not do what you think they should do and you are not able to carry out your chosen activity, and conversely how good it feels to be able to accomplish and improve your activities. Physical development must be demanding to be of some benefit. The stress produced must be controlled so that the influence on the tissues is beneficial; overstress is counterproductive and often harmful. The horse's natural temperament and attitude will give you indications as to the levels of mental and physical stress that he can cope with; he should 'bounce back' to his old self quickly after a rest and he should always be fully recovered before more demands are made. If in doubt, leave it out!

The Aims of the Development Programme

The basic aims of the development programme are for the horse to perform as well as his potential permits, to be as safe as possible for himself and his rider or driver, to be consistent in his work and to be able to go on working and performing for as long as possible. To accomplish this we need to develop:

- the horse's capacity to carry weight without losing any athletic ability
- our ability to control the horse with the lightest possible aids so that he is economical in his expenditure of effort and shows willingness, cooperation and obedience to the rider's demands. His trust in the rider will show in his pride in and enjoyment of his work
- the horse's ability to carry out gymnastic work such as jumping and galloping in a controlled way without any unnecessary fatigue
- his ability to make the best use of his balance and the full suppleness of his spine and limb joints, so that he can retain and confine his energy and release it in controlled, precise amounts.

Designing a Development Programme

To carry a rider efficiently, the horse must be developed to carry himself properly. Balance must be established first and then the carrying capacity of his hindquarters increased so that lumbosacral, sacroiliac, hip, stifle and hock joints can flex effectively to produce energy when required. This engagement of the hindquarters will allow the forehand to become lighter.

At the basic level, work should be aimed at improving the balanced posture. This is the result of encouraging the horse to stretch his total top line, not just by moving towards the ground but by raising his bottom line, thus shortening it by the correct use and progressive development of his abdominal group of muscles. These important muscles are at the root of many problems. If these muscles are under- or incorrectly developed, the horse cannot carry his gut adequately or hold up the base of his neck, round his back or engage his quarters effectively. Many so-called back problems are the result of slack muscles or lack of abdominal muscle development. These muscles should start their development before the horse is ridden, especially if it is weak or has a long back.

The abdominal group of muscles are attached to the sternum, ribs and the pubic bone of the pelvic girdle. This influences the horse's posture and his back support. The amount of development that can be obtained in this group of muscles will be determined by the degree of influence we can achieve over them, and that will be governed by the shape of the skeletal frame, the previous state of development, injuries and the trainer's skill and time. When these abdominal muscles are developed, the horse will be able to round his back and thus develop the lumbosacral joint to flex to engage his quarters, giving a strong supple back that can withstand the unnatural demands of carrying the rider without any loss of his athletic ability.

The terms 'on the bit' and 'degree of collection' are often used in dressage. Being 'on the bit' has little to do with the bit; it means that the horse has reached the degree of development that allows him a balanced posture and that he has the necessary strength and power for both engaging his hindquarters and elevating his forehand to carry out precise obedient movements. In racing, 'on the bit' is when the jockey wants the horse to take the bit and go; if he goes 'off the bridle', the horse has finished racing.

Remember that the horse was not designed to carry the 'compressed' weight of a rider but to carry the suspended weight of the huge gut and the foal. The horse is capable of carrying weight, but it will inhibit or restrict his forward movement and his ability to use himself to the best advantage. If the back muscles contract or shorten in the attempt to carry weight, they will become tight and sore making the horse hollow and unable to use his back. He will not develop his sling system which gives him flexibility and balance in turns. His back will sink between the scapulae, and the neck and head will be carried higher to compensate. This gives him a hollow back which cannot flex the lumbosacral joint so that the pelvis and quarters cannot engage. The hollow-backed horse is not easy to control, and the stress on the horse is so great that it can affect his temperament. The muscles of a sore back may not be too painful when blood is circulating through them during work; however, they can become very painful at rest in the stable when they have tightened and the circulation is restricted. This build-up of stress is cumulative and will wear the horse out prematurely.

There are a number of major muscles of the back, the largest being the longissimus which is segmental, meaning that its fibres contract in sequence. The back is not designed to remain rigid when in movement but to swing and pulsate. Anything that impedes this will reduce its suppleness and produce blockages in the transmission of energy which in turn will affect the horse's response and action. One of the important requirements of a performance horse is free forward movement: movement must be mentally and physically free with an even rhythm, and this can only be achieved if the horse has a supple back allowing its muscles to contract and stretch freely. In turn this can only happen if the abdominal group of muscles is well enough developed to give support to the back. As previously stated, these abdominal muscles are developed by encouraging the horse to stretch his top line down and raise his bottom line.

A criticism frequently made is that if the horse is allowed to go too deep in his work he will not come back up and get more and more on his forehand. However, if he is not allowed to stretch down, he will not stretch the muscles of his back and as we know from human athletic development this stretching is the first consideration. The degree that the horse will need to stretch down will depend on his skeletal shape and on the work you are going to ask for at a later stage. The horse that has the correct shape of neck for a dressage horse, of a correct length which fits into the body at an elevated position, will not need to go so deep to influence his abdominal muscles. In contrast the horse with a more horizontal neck set lower into his shoulder, perhaps with sharper curves in his neck bones, will need to stretch down further to influence his muscles. The latter conformation is associated with racehorses and he may be better doing other work than dressage.

What is happening to the muscles and the soft tissue that makes them change shape? Development involves strength, suppleness, power and endurance.

Suppleness, Strength and Power

A specific joint has a certain range or type of movement. The bones that make up the joints act as levers, and an arrangement of ligaments holds and balances the joints. These ligaments need to be stressed to develop their strength and at the same time the full range of movement of the joint in question must be maintained.

The angulation of the bones to each other will direct muscle pull on the body. The muscle groups which protect, move and moderate the gravitational pull on the joint must be supple enough to allow a full range of movement strong enough to prevent too much movement and powerful enough to produce the explosive force necessary to cause movement, lifting against gravity and moving the mass of the horse forwards. The bones that make up the joint are of different widths and lengths to allow for muscle attachment. The shape will determine whether the horse creates power or speed. Each muscle is made up of many fibres. If the muscles are asked to do light to medium work, a number of these fibres come into action. When they are tired others take over, and by the time the first fibres are asked to work again they are fully recovered. The harder the work load, the greater the number of fibres that are called into action at one time, and consequently the fibres work more frequently and fatigue will set in sooner.

Muscle fibres that are long are more designed to give a range of movement whereas shorter fibres produce power. To develop individual muscles to give suppleness, strength and endurance, the fibres need to be longer, not short, and with a well developed blood supply and a good ability to work aerobically. Look at the Grand National or long-distance horse: he is lean and strong whereas the sprinter has bulky, powerful muscles.

The individual muscle fibres of powerful muscles are more bulky and the muscle is shorter and tighter, reducing the range of movement. These short, tight, powerful muscles develop more from the short explosive work and will develop muscle mass. The fibres can develop in muscle from resistance and can be the cause of muscle imbalance, giving rise to bulky curves. For example, the horse that resists the action of the rider's hands will build up muscle at the poll which prevents him from being able to flex with softness. It also causes him discomfort when his rider asks him to flex at the poll.

Basic development consists of preparing the soft tissue to ensure adequate strength, suppleness and good posture. The endurance work or power development will come after the basic work. For the degree of collection and engagement necessary for successful showjumping and dressage, the horse will need power to execute the work required. However, the stayer — the steeplechaser or the event horse — needs less bulk to carry around at speed and more suppleness to get over fences at a gallop. The long-distance horse needs endurance and strength with as little bulk to carry around as possible.

Endurance is enhanced by aerobic work which encourages the horse's ability to supply oxygen to the muscle cells and improves the muscle's precision, range, strength and endurance in action and posture. Muscle power is built up by anaerobic exercise, the kind that exercises the muscles very intensively for a brief period of time, perhaps only for seconds. You can see why this type of development follows *after* the basic development.

Power development in young horses can produce problems in the skeletal structures. The bone of young growing horses is very resilient and adaptable but, during training, muscle, tendons and ligaments can become stronger and more elastic than the growing bone can cope with. This can cause bony problems in young horses, especially in the epiphyseal cartilages which are at their weakest towards the end of the growing period. Any excessive stress on these growth plates will stop growth at the end where the problem occurs while the other end carries on growing, and of course the opposite limb continues to grow. If the stress or injury is extreme, skeletal imbalances, for example differences in leg length, may be the result.

There are a great many books that will show you the correct techniques that aid the basic development programme. The methods include lungeing, long reining, loose schooling, ridden work and the use of different tack and equipment. All of them concentrate on improving the horse's balance and gait, his rhythm and elasticity, his coordination and his response to your instructions.

If you are getting despondent and think that all this is quite beyond you, take heart. Someone known to one of the authors achieved a very supple, straight and balanced horse that displayed excellent posture and elastic gaits using nothing but walking up hills and ridge-and-furrow and a minimum of trot and canter work with the occasional 'pop' if an obstacle happened to be in the way. This was first carried out on the lunge line and long reins and then under saddle. The idea was to ensure that the horse walked correctly with different degrees of contact and was always straight and active, with the rhythm and balance maintained in circles and turns, up hill and down hill and across slopes. Walking over raised poles and through mazes, and on different surfaces with different depths of going, was incorporated into the programme as the horse's balance improved.

Of course this rider was a well balanced rider who could influence her horse correctly and was very consistent in maintaining the horse's activity; once she was on board and gave the aids, the horse had to go forward into a very active walk and she never allowed the horse to use the walk as a rest while she was riding it. She would jump from the horse and walk beside it or stop occasionally as a reward. This horse had excellent posture, even development and good balance, and was calm, very forward going and straight.

Not all of us have this talent, dedication or time. Don't worry: there are many ways to carry out this development work and they can be adapted to your way of living, your ability and the amount of professional help available. It is important to plan how you will programme the work, bearing in mind where you will need help, what time you can spare, which are the best exercises, what you will need, and the best area or place to work.

Write down your objectives clearly, be positive, and of course have your horse's profile at hand as a base from which to start.

What is Development?

Development is reshaping the horse's posture to the 'shape' he needs to carry your weight economically and athletically. The amount of time you will need to impose this 'shape' on your horse will depend on:

- the degree of development needed for your particular sport
- his stage of development at the start
- his basic structure

The 'shape' that we have in mind as the ideal can sometimes be misleading depending on our prejudices and experience. Picture a horse being ridden in front of you. He displays what looks like a good shape, but on close inspection his posture is poor, his action is heavy and earth-bound, and he is not athletic. His naturally rounded top line leads us to believe that he is well developed, so this horse is expected to perform as well as a horse which has undergone a development programme. These unfortunate horses are usually naturally athletic but are not developed correctly and never fulfil their potential. We have come across many horses like these which begin to have problems in their backs and their stifles and have to be redeveloped.

When looking at a horse, analyse his shape, posture and action, how he carries the rider, the swing in his back, his under line and the position of his hips. They are all clues as to his degree of development. The most difficult thing a horse has to do is to carry and balance a rider on his back and be controlled by him. The horse naturally carries more weight on his forehand. The weight of the rider adds to this, and we cannot expect him to be athletic with this added weight and change of balance unless we change his posture and the distribution of his weight. If we do not, his front limbs and feet will suffer prematurely.

The important aspects to develop are:

(1) the balancing of body weight
(2) the length and or power of the stride
(3) the weight-carrying capacity
(4) athletic dexterity

An examination of the near perfect frame at the basic stage and comparison with your own horse's measurements will show you how much work there is to do. The whole horse must be balanced: in the skeletal frame, in his development and in his feet, and where there are imbalances we must work towards improvement. The development programme does not aim to make your horse conform to a set standard or shape but to develop his posture and to bring him into balance so that he can work in comfort and move as well as possible.

The measurements you will have to take from your horse's profile are:

(1) The size and the shape of the feet: the size must be correct in relation to the horse and must give balanced equal support so that the stress is shared by all the parts (see Fig. 3.11).
(2) The balance and alignment of the limb bones: the better aligned these are, the more the foot will take a balanced weight and hence there is less stress on the bones and the soft tissues (see Fig. 3.7).

(3) The base of support: the relation of the point of shoulder to the position of the elbow and the stifle to the hock will influence the placement of the foot and the support of the body and consequently the distribution of stress (Fig. 4.2).

(4) The weight and the length of the head: the head acts as a balancing pole so, the heavier the head, the shorter the neck must be to carry it (Fig. 3.8).

(5) The length and the shape of the neck (Figs 4.1, 4.5, 4.6, 4.7): the shape is more important than the length in some activities. The neck vertebrae should present two, equal, loose curves, one at the top and one at the bottom. If the curve is too steep at the top of the neck, the horse will be peacocky; if too shallow, it will not be able to flex well. The position of the attachment of the neck to the body is important; if the lower curve is steep, the neck is positioned low in relation to the shoulders and the horse will find it hard to raise his head and neck without hollowing his back and becoming ewe-necked. This type of horse will not be best suited to dressage, but the neck will respond to development work given time. The development work will mainly improve the correct function of the scalenus muscles which give the arch to the root of the neck. Many horses look ewe-necked because they have not been developed in a good posture. In such animals the abdominal muscles are weak so that the body has hollowed, the back has sunk between the scapulae and the neck has braced itself to help the horse to carry the rider and itself. In a bad case the only way

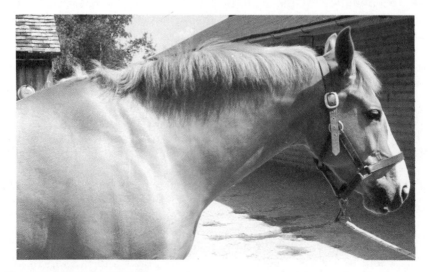

Fig. 4.5 A short thick neck.

Fig. 4.6 A large brachiocephalic muscle.

Fig. 4.7 Correct development has overcome the problem shown in Fig. 4.6.

to redevelop the neck is to get off his back and reposture him by encouraging him to learn to carry himself correctly.

(6)   The length of the horse from the point of shoulder to point of buttock (Fig. 3.7). Ideally the height of the horse is equal to or slightly less than his length. Asking a short horse to round himself and shorten even further can take him out of balance, making it difficult to develop him well. You must bear in mind how important are the parts that make up this length and their relations to each other. If the middle of the back is long, it means that the front and hind parts may be short and the back vulnerable. If the mid back is shorter, then the front and the hind parts are probably better. It may be that either the front end or the hindquarter is superior, causing a balance problem. The mid back should be nearly horizontal behind the wither to a slightly raised loin giving strength to the lumbar area. The last rib to the sacrum should be long enough for good muscle attachment but not too long as this will wear the lumbosacral joint due to the longer lever action upon it. The longer the rib cage the shorter the loin, and conversely the shorter the rib cage the longer the loin and the weaker the back and the lumbosacral joint. If the mid back is short overall, it will be less supple and mobility will be reduced, and the fibrocartilage discs may be shorter and will not absorb enough movement. The limbs on such horses may be very active and take a lot of the strain. If the back is long, it may have too much flexibility setting up problems in the back and making such horses uncomfortable to ride; development is needed to protect this type of back. A long back may restrict the forward reach of the hind limb so that the lumbosacral joint is not used to engage the quarters and the muscles are not used fully. These horses are hard to develop as it is difficult to influence the abdominal muscles to bring the pelvis forwards in the correct posture. If the skeletal conformation is good but the back is short and tight, the horse must be slowly encouraged to stretch the back muscles to soften them and allow the circulation to flow efficiently. If force is used to stretch the back, it can pull on the bony attachments and the joints and do immense harm.

(7)   The height at the withers (Fig. 3.4): this should be equal to the length, or a fraction shorter, to ensure balance.

(8)   Height at the croup (Fig. 3.4): this can be the same as the height at the withers; however, if the withers are higher, the seating for the saddle is better and there will be less concussion and compression on the limbs because the centre of

mass is further to the rear. This consideration is not as important for the horse that will not carry weight for long periods of time as it is for the hunter which may carry a heavy weight for many hours. As before the effect will depend on the parts of the whole height; the deeper the withers to girth measurement the more weight the horse can balance and carry. A high croup with a shallow girth will find carrying weight a big problem and will need a great deal more time and effort to develop any degree of athletic ability while carrying a rider. A high croup may be due to the angulation of the hind limbs which can make the speed potential greater as seen in some racehorses. You must determine by your measurements whether the withers are low or the croup is high.

(9)   Position of the withers: This is perhaps one of the most important aspects of performance and balance. As we have mentioned, the withers should continue from the neck to finish near to the mid back. The curve should be smooth with no pits or sharp dips and be neither too sharp and high nor too thick and low. The shoulder length and angulation (Fig. 3.7) will be a determining factor in the balance and activity of the horse. The angle of the scapula to the horizontal and the angle of the humerus to the horizontal may be slightly different; the total angle between the two bones at the shoulder joint should be approximately 110°. The difference in placement of scapula and humerus will give rise to certain differences in the action; the more upright the humerus and the more angulated the scapula the greater the stride length, whereas the straighter the scapula in relation to the humerus the greater the elevation.

(10)   The croup and the hind limb (Fig. 3.6): your measurement of the pelvis and stifle will indicate the type of stride, the power or endurance and the degree of angulation to the horizontal and to each other. The total length of the croup is the measurement of the ilium and the ischium and will indicate stride length, an important measurement in any athlete especially the galloping horse. The longer the ischium the greater the area for muscle attachment. The slope of the croup, i.e. the point of hip (the tuber coxae) to the point of seat bone (the tuber ischium) will determine the type of stride; the more horizontal croup has less pulling power but a light, swinging stride giving little fatigue which is ideal for long-distance horses. The more sloping croup gives more power. The angulation of the hip joint (the ilium and the femur) should be approximately 90°. If less than this, the stifle joint will be

placed forwards with good muscle attachment, and if the angle is more than 90°, the stifle will lie to the rear. The length and the slope of the femur and tibia are also important: a long, moderately sloping femur will help in speed and jumping and can affect balance. A shorter, sloping femur will give more upwards movement rather than extension. A good balance of femur and tibia is therefore more important in dressage horses. When the tibia is more sloping, the angle of the hind limb becomes more closed and the body and hindquarters will be more greatly influenced. (The stifles and the hocks work together when the foot is off the ground.) The hock that is close to the ground will give short strong cannon bones. The hock should also be large and strong to accommodate a good insertion of the Achilles tendon.

(11) The position of the centre of mass: if the centre of mass is too far forward, the horse will be on his forehand and more development work will be needed to relieve the forehand of this greater weight. If the centre of mass is too far back, this will put a lot of strain on to the important lumbosacral joint with undesirable effects.

(12) The bone measurement (Fig. 3.8): this is an estimate of the strength available to support the body. This strength is related to the length of the cannon bone as well as to its circumference; a short, strong cannon bone will compensate for lack of bone but if the horse has long cannon bones and lacks bone measurement it may indicate a weakness, particularly if the horse is tied-in below the knee. The knees should be as close to the ground as possible, and substantial but not round.

5
Specialist development

Equipment and Techniques Used for Development and Rehabilitation

After the development or rehabilitation programme has been planned from an in-depth study of the horse in question, it must be decided what tack or equipment, if any, should be used for the ground schooling exercises without the weight of the rider. The objectives should be listed, and the various methods of applying the tack must be understood. With the information you have collected about your horse, you are beginning to build up a mental picture of how he is put together and how, with careful development and monitoring, you can aid his development.

The Use of Specialist Tack — Why?

The main reason for specialist tack is not to tie up, restrict or force the horse into a particular outline. The whole concept of development is to mould the body so that it will develop the shape that is best suited for ease of work, economy of action and prevention of occupational stress and strain, and that will give a prolonged working life in all the different disciplines.

A horse with a near perfect skeletal structure, carefully developed in his breaking or starting programme, progressively schooled and competed in the ideal way, and never suffering lameness or injury that would alter his way of performing, is a rare animal indeed. Few of us will ever find this perfection, and, if we did, it might prove somewhat boring!

The normal horse is one with his own unique personality and problems, and his skeletal shape is probably less than perfect. His starting or breaking may have been rushed, or perhaps his developmental progress may have been interrupted by injury or curtailed to acommodate the owner's time schedule. Maybe the body movement has never been corrected after injury, and incorrect development has left its mark in the form of bad posture.

Sometimes the horse may have developed an incorrect shape because of a psychological problem in an effort to protect himself or from fear and apprehension. This protection may have created tension in many muscles, especially those of the back, resulting in a tense tight back which, if required to extend under the weight of a rider, will cause pain. The horse may come to associate this pain with a rider or ridden work. A chain reaction can occur and the point may be reached at which the horse cannot take any more and rebels. This chain reaction must be broken.

The old riding masters talked about 'Calm, forward and straight' as the initial criteria in the development of the horse. 'Calm' is always first in order of importance. Without this inner peace and security, without the confidence in himself and in his trainer, all effort will be for nothing.

Back and neck pain is common in human beings, and much of this is attributable to poor posture and the way we carry out our everyday activities. These minor effects can be cumulative, eventually leading to severe pain. On seeking advice we may be advised to undertake a programme of exercises designed to counteract the effects of our activities and to correct our posture. Because these exercises involve changing reflexes that have become firmly established, it is not an easy thing to do without help and will involve a lot of effort, time and commitment.

Relating this to the horse you will see that, because we cannot discuss his postural problem with him, any remedial treatment has to be imposed. But how should it be imposed? It must be done with care, understanding and an appreciation that remedial treatment involves careful development not the use of force. If force is used, the horse will either compensate elsewhere or he will resist and any resistance will only develop the muscles incorrectly. Remedial work is carried out to encourage the horse to rediscover his natural balance, to develop his degree of engagement and to make supple any part of his body that has become tight from past resistances or overdevelopment. It may be possible for the very knowledgeable and talented rider to change this posture and movement under saddle. Few, however, possess such a high degree of talent or ability, and even then riding may not be the best form of rehabilitation for the horse.

The tack that we will discuss is for use in developing the horse and not as an aid to control him. If development tack is used, keep in mind the principle that the horse is made to feel more comfortable when he responds correctly, and is caused discomfort if he responds incorrectly. If done progressively, little and often, it will improve his way of moving and his ability to carry himself properly.

The results that tack produces depend upon the ability of the person using it. Tack should be used to *encourage* the correct responses and influence the correct development. If the tack does not help to encourage the horse to produce the action required, however good the piece of tack is supposed to be it will not help this particular horse's development.

Various items of tack that can be of use in ground schooling to influence the posture, self-carriage and movement include side reins, running reins, the chambon, the Carlburg, the equi-lunge and the equi-weight. The scrawbrig bridle will also be included as it too can help with development problems, although it is normally used for ridden work to re-establish confidence in the hands or the bit after development has been corrected.

We should remind ourselves that correct posture is required to free the back from any tightness so that the horse can stretch the back and the neck. The abdominal muscles must be developed to carry the gut and to support the back. The abdominal muscles have their attachment areas at one end on the pubic bone of the pelvic girdle and at the other to the sternum, so this carrying of the gut will incline the pelvis and the hindquarters underneath the body thus shortening the base of support. The important muscles that produce the elevation of the forehand and give a *firm* support to the base of the neck are also influenced by the correct action of the abdominal muscles. Unrestricted, balanced, forward movement will ensure that the sling system is also developed to free the shoulders' action and ensure their equal suppleness.

It is important to remember that there is a thin line between asking and encouraging a horse to try a certain action, even if uncomfortable, and forcing him to do something. The trainer must respond to the reactions of the horse, doing only enough to stress the tissues and thus influence the body without overstress. We are seeking the horse's cooperation, and this will depend upon how well he can take this imposition both physically and mentally. Any part of the body that feels fatigue will seek to compensate for the action imposed. If this happens, we will simply be developing the compensation and the muscles' tightness. The minute any compensation is produced, or preferably before, the demand must stop and only be reintroduced following different exercise. If the horse resists the correct action because it hurts too much or because he cannot do what you wish, an incorrect shape will develop. He will be happy to give of his best for short periods, even if he is uncomfortable, after which he should be rewarded by being given time to stretch and relax in between demands and a change of exercise.

Where Should Development Take Place?

Where the remedial development is to be carried out needs to be considered. Remember: you are trying to influence the horse to accept impositions while readjusting his posture and thus his movement. It is therefore essential to find an area where there is a minimum of distraction. If the horse becomes tense or excited during his rehabilitation work, this will be counterproductive and a waste of your time. You will only be developing or increasing the tenseness. The ideal area is one that is enclosed, quiet and tranquil, an area where you and your horse can become as one; an area for meditation. In a philosophy study, an interpretation of meditation given to one of the authors was 'working in harmony'. Your harmony will affect the horse so he becomes calm and responsive and part of you. If you are conscious of the presence of other people or of the telephone ringing, this harmony will be unobtainable so find a peaceful place. Ten minutes' concentrated effort is worth many hours of ordinary work. Some prefer to work completely alone so that the horse has only to respond to one person and there is no danger of his getting confused. If you wish to have another person on hand either from a safety point of view or because you need help to adjust equipment, they must remain absolutely still and quiet. A good assistant will automatically know what is needed, and his or her questions and discussion will come later and should be helpful in preparing for the next session.

The area where the work is to be carried out needs to be a ring of approximately 20 m diameter. 'Play pens' of this size can now be purchased. It is desirable to have the sides totally enclosed to prevent distraction or optical illusions. This 'pen' can be used for lungeing, long-reining and loose schooling, incorporating the use of any necessary tack. Collapsible poles with interchangeable heights can be built into the sides of the ring. They can be fitted for walking pace — approximately 85–100 cm (2 ft 9 in to 3 ft 3 in) apart, and at the other side for trotting poles placed approximately 130–145 cm (4 ft 3 in to 4 ft 9 in) apart. These poles must be adjusted to suit the individual horse so that his natural rhythm is not lost. The number of poles to be used at any session will depend on what you are hoping to achieve and upon the horse's physical and mental capabilities. The surface in the ring needs to be firm and even, with some spring and a slight slope to provide good drainage. The advantage of the 'play pen' is that it can be moved regularly, and if you have good, sandy, well drained soil you may not need any other additional surface. Harrow the area after the pen has been moved so that it becomes firm and even again for later use. A lane for remedial pole work can be a useful addition.

What Type of Tack?

Side reins (Fig. 5.1)

Side reins can be plain or have either elastic or rubber inserts. These reins are fitted from the saddle or the roller to the bit rings or cavesson.

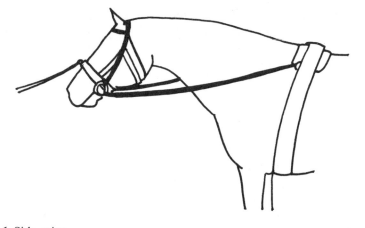

Fig. 5.1 Side reins.

The fitting to the roller or the saddle can be high or low but should not be lower than the point of shoulder. The fitting will be dictated by the horse's conformation, his response to the side reins and what you hope to achieve by their use. The side reins will need to be lower if the horse has a poorly set-on neck than if he has the widest part of his neck higher in relation to his chest.

The main aim of using side reins is to encourage the horse to reach down and seek contact with the bit. Reaching down will extend the back and help to stretch the top of the neck. Side reins will have an influence on the inside hind leg action by increasing flexion and reducing overextension. This influence is particularly important in horses with weak or underdeveloped stifle joints. If a horse with weak stifle joints is allowed to run or overextend, these joints may lock and the soft tissue would be damaged. This may be an initial cause of problems in the stifle area which appear later in the horse's schooling, especially in extended movements. Increased flexion will encourage the hindquarters to come further under the body, which will help to raise the horse's back just behind the saddle area. Rounding of the back is accomplished by the increased effort of the abdominal muscles and the lumbosacral joint.

The length of the side reins is of great importance and should be adjusted for the different exercises and for each horse depending on his specific problem and his overall development. Length should also be adjusted according to the objective you are aiming towards, the gait the horse is working in, the demands you are imposing on the horse and whether the horse is warmed up or is cooling down. The main indication of the correct length is that the horse is moving forwards freely without restriction and at the same time using the back and hind limbs effectively. Side reins will need to be longer at the walk and canter and slightly shorter at the trot. If the posture of the horse is imposed by shortening the side reins, the gaits will suffer and this will not bring the desired results. Correct action should be asked for in very short, well defined stints. The rhythm and activity are maintained by good use of voice, your position and the use of the lunge whip.

If the horse is not stretching down and seeking the bit, a change of bit may be all that is necessary for him to respond properly. For example, jointed snaffles can bruise the roof of the horse's mouth and a change to a mullen-mouth bit may prevent this.

If the horse still evades contact with the bit and is not stretching his back, and if a full mouth assessment and veterinary investigations find no physical cause, then running side reins should be tried. These give more lateral freedom.

Running side reins (Fig. 5.2)

These are an alternative to fixed side reins and many people prefer the greater freedom they give. Two reins, longer than side reins, are fitted so that they pass from the sides of the girth or roller to and through the bit rings and back again to the roller. Running side reins can also be fitted together, making one long rein (make sure they are adjusted to the correct length) coming from one side of the roller/saddle, through the same side bit ring, over the poll, to the bit ring on the other side and back to the saddle/roller (Fig. 5.4). This rein is put on quite loosely to start with, and adjusted as the horse becomes aware of its action

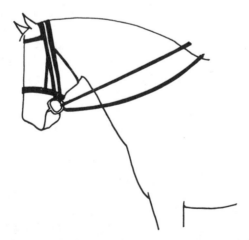

Fig. 5.2 Running side reins. Running reins and draw reins are frequently used on ridden horses for developmental purposes. They are more effective when used on the lunge as the horse is free to use its back without the weight of the rider.

so that it is taken up progressively to give gentle contact. This can also encourage the horse to stretch down. Running reins are very effective for the more experienced horse which has developed incorrectly. Again, as with all other side reins, they are used after the horse has been warmed up and for brief periods between other demands. It is just like doing any exercises, building up slowly the time and the duration, allowing the tissues time to develop.

Care must be exercised in the use of side reins, especially in the walk. The natural swing of this gait should not be lost and the reins must be adjusted to maintain this.

Some trainers consider that fixed side reins should not be used at the walk. Running side reins are a useful alternative. These reins must not be mistaken for draw reins which incorporate a lever action because of their fitting, from between the horse's front legs through the bit rings and back to the roller (Figs 5.3 and 5.4).

Side reins are frequently used for control, particularly when lungeing a horse in an open field or perhaps when putting a rider on the lunge. In remedial work the side reins are never put on to maintain control. If you need more control, the side reins can be fitted to the cavesson. You must never put yourself in a position in which the horse is not controllable: he could hurt himself and make his problems worse. You must always be one step ahead of the horse; anticipate his actions and reactions and counter-react. Never put yourself in a position in which the horse can take advantage of you or the situation. Be firm, be positive, concentrate. Always keep a contact on the cavesson so

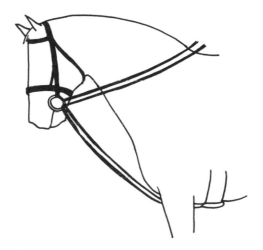

Fig. 5.3 Draw reins fitted between the forelegs. Reins taken from the girth through the bit to the roller or the rider's hands, usually referred to as draw reins, can be useful but can stiffen the rhomboideus and the trapezius muscles if fitted too tightly.

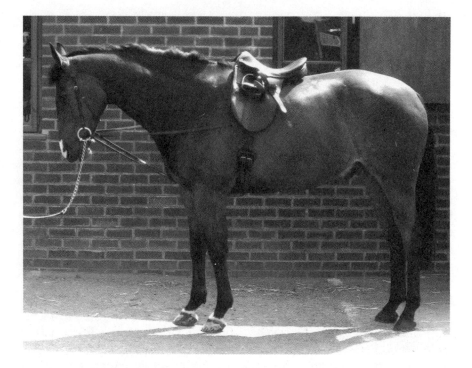

Fig. 5.4 Draw reins can be used as one long rein from side girth to bit, to girth between legs, back to the bit on the opposite side and to side girth.

you pick up the senses of the horse. Keep eye contact with the horse even when sorting or adjusting your tack or looking at his action. Your vision must include his eyes and his ears.

If you are going to develop the horse mentally or physically on the ground, you need to have a confined area as previously described. This will eliminate the need for forced control.

The Carlburg (Figs 5.5 and 5.6)

This piece of tack is especially useful for correcting developmental problems, for example in the horse with an overdeveloped forehand which he has used to propel himself forward instead of using his hind-quarters to push himself forward. Horses that are low in the withers, that are croup high or that have a low neck setting to the shoulders can be supported and encouraged to lift and lighten their forehand by use of the Carlburg. This lightening of the forehand will help the horse to carry himself in a more balanced way. The use of the Carlburg may have to be repeated periodically to support the development of a horse with these structural problems.

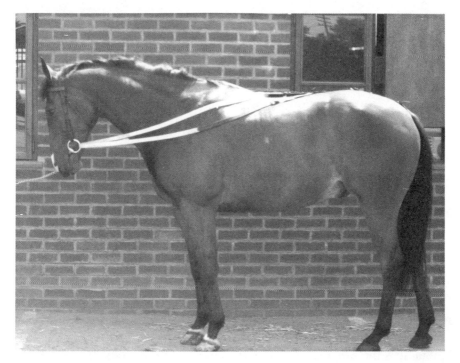

Fig. 5.5 Carlburg.

Fig. 5.6 Carlburg.

The crupper and back strap have three elastic straps with buckles; the reins are usually of web, having a central strap which is fastened to the central buckle of the back strap and lies across the withers then divides into two, each rein passing through the bit rings and back to the two remaining straps on the back strap. This works on the principle that if the horse leans on his bit it will put pressure on his dock. The horse will tuck his hindquarters under him and carry himself instead of leaning heavily on his forehand.

The chambon (Fig. 5.7)

This piece of tack can be used to develop the horse by encouraging him to stretch down and round his back. It is also very effective in freeing the sling system. The chambon can only achieve this if the back is correctly influenced when the horse stretches down. It must be introduced so that at first it does not influence the horse at all. When the horse has accepted its presence, the strings can be adjusted a little each day. This way the exercise gradually builds up and the horse is not forced to go in a certain way.

So, how tight to fit it? The answer is to fit the chambon so that it just influences the horse's way of going. If your horse looks happy and his work gives a good picture, that will probably be the correct fitting. In a week's time you may find that it can be adjusted a little more and so on. As a rehabilitation aid the chambon helps the horse to re-establish his own balance and reduce any tight resistances he has developed through compensation.

Some animals, usually horses with long necks and low neck settings

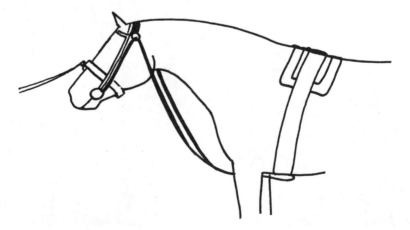

Fig. 5.7 Chambon fitted for lungeing. It should not be fitted more tightly to fix the horse in a low outline.

to their shoulders, can move along with their noses to the ground in the chambon without stretching or influencing their backs at all. If this tack is not having any effect on the muscular system, there is no point in using it. There are other ways of achieving this, perhaps without using tack at all.

The chambon, if used as part of a development or rehabilitation programme, can improve the development of a lot of horses. It helps to develop the muscles that aid in raising the root of the neck, the scalenus muscles, which will help to flex the poll and to stretch the top line.

It is good practice to use a rubber bit when first introducing a chambon. If your horse has a very tight, wooden back, it is best not to use a chambon until the back has been treated with soft tissue manipulation. The reason is that if you are asking the horse to stretch and extend his back when it is short and tight, it may damage the important lumbosacral joint. Any strain on this joint is serious from a performance point of view. This is even more important if your horse has a long lumbar span and is higher in the croup that at the withers. If your horse has had any sacroiliac strain, the chambon must be used with great care. It may not be the best tack to use in these cases.

The chambon is fitted as a martingale, through the girth, and it divides into two strings which go through rings or pulleys attached to the headpiece of the bridle; they are then clipped on to the bit rings. Once again the idea is to encourage the horse to reach down and raise his back. If the head and neck are raised, pressure is put on to his mouth. When he lowers his head and neck he feels more comfortable. It is important to remember that the tack should be used after the horse has been warmed up and has settled down. It should only be used for short durations, increasing as the horse's body adjusts to the demands. We like to use it at slow gaits: walk, trot and slow canter.

The Equi-lunge (Fig. 5.8)

The equi-lunge has similar effects to the pieces of tack mentioned previously, and is used both for development and for the correction of development problems. With some horses we prefer to use it in place of a chambon as it is not quite so restricting. It can also be used for leading and ridden work.

The Equi-weight

The equi-weight (Fig. 5.9) consists of a chain bearing a variable number of weights. This is fastened at either end to each bit ring, and hangs below the jaw. The same principle as for the equi-lunge applies: when the horse feels uncomfortable from the weight on his bars, he will drop

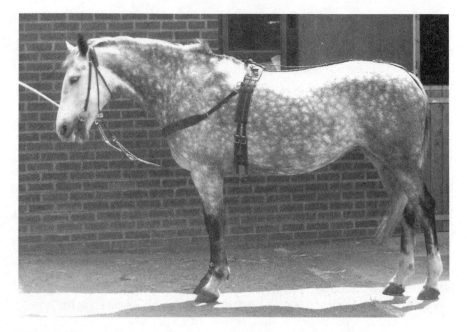

Fig. 5.8 The equi-lunge can be used as side reins for a developed horse, or like German draw reins it works on the back and can aid posture development, and can be used for riding, lungeing and long reining.

Fig. 5.9 Equi-weight.

his head to a more vertical position affecting his neck and back, as has been described earlier. This will also help to prevent resistance in the jaw against the bit.

The Scrawbrig Bridle (Figs 5.10–5.12)

This is particularly useful if a horse has a mouth problem. Remember that a mouth problem can cause the horse to develop incorrectly due to compensation caused by discomfort or pain in his mouth. Once a mouth problem has been resolved and the necessary work has been carried out to restore the back to full function, then the scrawbrig bridle can be of great value in re-establishing confidence in the bit. It consists of a conventional headpiece with throatlash and cheekpieces supporting a padded noseband with strong side rings. This noseband looks very similar to a drop noseband but is fitted slightly larger. In

Fig. 5.10 A scrawbrig bitless bridle.

Fig. 5.11 Scrawbrig.

Fig. 5.12 Scrawbrig.

the chin groove is another padded section, tapering to reins which pass through the side rings and to the rider's hand.

This bridle has three fittings which are used in progression. The first part of the system is used for control via the nose and the bottom jaw (Fig. 5.10). The second part, added later, includes a head piece with a bit attached, but this is not used for control, which still comes from the nose and bottom jaw (Fig. 5.11). The third element includes an extra rein, which is attached to the bit (Fig. 5.12). This rein is used for a short time each day, and contact with the bit is gradually increased until confidence has been restored. This is not the same as a hackamore, which applies lever action to the head. For safety reasons it is better to use the scrawbrig bridle in an enclosed area as the control is not from the bit.

De Gogue (Fig. 5.13)

The de Gogue is a type of schooling martingale which comes in two patterns, the independent and the command. The principle is the same in both cases, namely to induce correct head carriage by putting pressure on the poll and the bars of the mouth.

Control head collars

The *Equi-col* (Fig. 5.14) is a type of head collar which can be adjusted to fit any horse. Consequently it fits well and gives good control. It is useful at shows or in company when you need to put on or remove a bridle in an open area as you never lose control of the horse for a crucial time as with a conventional head collar.

The '*Be Nice*' head collar (Fig. 5.15) is popular is America. It gives a high degree of control and can be used to teach the young horse to lead

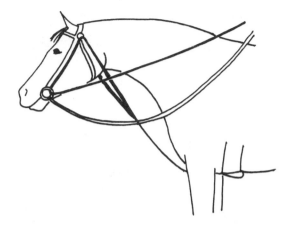

Fig. 5.13 A Gogue fitted for riding.

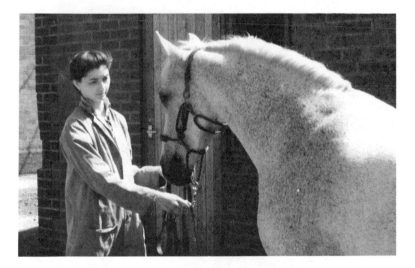

Fig. 5.14 Control head collar. Equi-col can be useful as you can adjust it to fit many different horses so it fits well and gives good control. It can be used to put on or remove a bridle without any movement when the horse is not under control. Very useful if in company or at shows, etc., with an exposed area.

correctly. If he behaves well he will be comfortable. However, if he misbehaves he can be punished on the poll, nose and chin by a quick jerk on the head collar rope.

Martingales

There are many martingales available and most are used to stop the horse from placing his head above the point of control. The most sim-

Fig. 5.15 The 'Be Nice' head collar.

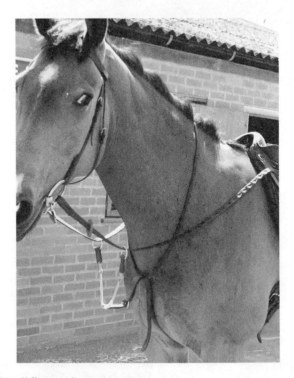

Fig. 5.16 The sliding and running martingale.

Fig. 5.17 Balancing rein.

ple forms are the standing martingale and the running martingale, which are in common use. The more complicated Market Harborough may be classified as a martingale or a rein as it is in fact both. It consists of a rein clipped to the snaffle rein which passes back through the ring of the snaffle and attaches to what is in effect a very short standing martingale. When the horse stiffens his poll and jaw and raises his head the rein comes into play; the pressure on the bit makes him lower his head which gives instant relief.

The simple running martingale in Fig. 5.16 is useful. It has a non-fixed cord attached to the reins which gives freedom in turns and is much less restricting. If used in the wrong way, a running martingale can cause the horse to carry his head incorrectly resulting in poor development.

Balancing reins (Fig. 5.17)

These are rather controversial schooling aids designed to help the horse find his own balance by lowering his head and neck and stretching his back. There is no doubt that skilled and experienced people can use these reins with great effect, but poorly used they can do more harm than good.

Girths, Rollers and Surcingles

It is worth including girths, rollers and surcingles in this section as so many horses have muscle problems in this area. Injuries to the sternum and ribs can leave areas of poor circulation resulting in tight and sore muscle and connective tissue. Girthing up can consequently be quite uncomfortable for the horse although once the horse has warmed up these areas become less uncomfortable.

Overgirthing resulting in excess pressure on the pectoral muscles can cause lumpy areas in the muscle and connective tissue of the chest and between the fore limbs. Galloping and jumping necessitate a tight girth and the horse may seem short-strided in front the day after exertion. He will resent the girth being done up and may be mistaken for being cold backed. Each horse's barrel is a different shape and it is important to choose a girth that gives even pressure overall, not a pinpoint pressure. The round-chested horse will take good all-round pressure whereas the more pear-shaped horse will tend to feel pressure in one area. Try not to girth up your horse too tightly, and let him warm up before pulling the girth up that extra hole.

6
Routine care of the equine athlete

Nutrition

An essential ingredient of any successful training programme is correct feeding to ensure that the horse's demand for vital nutrients is met by a palatable ration.

The Vital Nutrients

In order to design a balanced ration it is necessary to understand what nutrients the horse requires and how he uses these to create what we are looking for, namely energy for movement. The six necessary ingredients of the horse's diet are carbohydrates, protein, fat, minerals, vitamins and water.

Carbohydrates

Sugars, starch and cellulose are all examples of carbohydrates. Some, such as glucose, have a very simple structure and are very easily digested; others, like cellulose, which makes up plant cell walls, are complex and consequently very difficult to digest. The horse is designed to eat grass which has a very high cellulose or insoluble carbohydrate content. To overcome the problems of digesting this cellulose the horse's gut has become highly specialised (Figs 6.1 and 6.2). The horse's hind gut, consisting of the caecum, large colon and small colon, is large compared with that of, say, a dog or man, and houses a vast population of micro-organisms. These bugs live on the cellulose which has passed virtually unaltered through the horse's stomach and small intestine. As they extract the nutrients they require, the bugs produce, by a process of fermentation, substances which are absorbed by the horse's gut and are used to produce energy. This cosy set-up gives the micro-organisms a warm, dark, safe environment and a constant intake of food, and the horse gains nutrition from an otherwise virtually indigestible part of the diet.

The cereal part of the horse's ration provides soluble carbohydrates

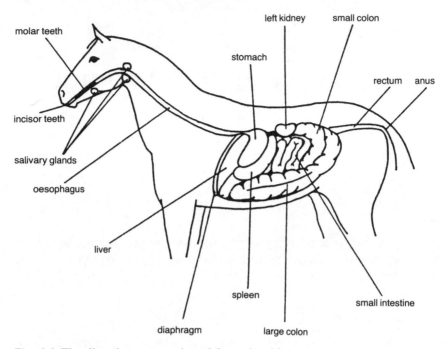

Fig. 6.1 The digestive system viewed from the side

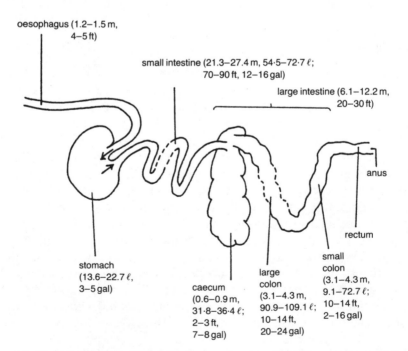

Fig. 6.2 The alimentary canal of the horse, showing dimensions and capacities of different regions.

such as sugars and starch which are broken down in the small intestine and absorbed into the bloodstream. Any not used immediately for energy production is stored in the liver and muscles for future use.

Carbohydrates, either as cereals or roughage, form the largest part of the horse's diet and serve to provide the horse with energy. Consequently carbohydrates are particularly important in the performance horse.

Measuring the energy in food

Most of us at some time have squeezed into a pair of jeans and thought, 'Oh dear, time to go on a diet!' The correct way to diet is to design a balanced ration of a limited number of calories, in other words, one that gives a limited energy intake. These days even the label on your yoghurt pot tells you how many calories you are eating. Look more closely at the pot. The energy value is not only given in calories but also in joules; joule is the metric energy unit just as centimetre is the metric unit of linear measurement and inch the imperial unit. The energy value of horse feeds is measured in megajoules (MJ). Oats contain about 14 MJ of digestible energy (DE) per kilogram (kg) whereas cubes may only contain 10 MJ DE per kg. You would have to feed 1.5 kg of cubes to supply your horse with the same amount of energy as 1 kg oats; conversely 0.7 kg oats would replace 1 kg cubes.

The energy requirement of your horse will depend on many factors but principally his size and the amount of work that he is doing. Once these are known it is fairly simple to work out his energy requirements in terms of megajoules per day, and hence how much feed he must receive. Think back to your diet book in which you are given a table, and, depending on your height, build and lifestyle, you are allocated a certain number of calories a day. We shall do this later for your horse.

Protein

Protein makes up the majority of body tissue in forms as diverse as muscle and hair and hoof. Consequently, protein is needed in the diet for body building and tissue repair. Proteins are made of 25 different building blocks called amino acids. These can be thought of as being like the letters of the alphabet; letters are put together in different sequences to form words that have a certain meaning. Amino acids are put together to form proteins that have different functions. This is why proteins can have such diverse forms and functions. The amino acid content of a protein determines that protein's 'quality'. Lots of 'a's' put together do not make a word, and, similarly, amino acids must be present in the diet in balanced amounts. The amino acids lysine and methionine are the two most likely to be in short supply in a horse fed a traditional diet of oats, bran and hay. This deficiency upsets the balance of amino acids in the diet and disrupts the body's metabolism, for example by restricting growth rate. Consequently methionine and lysine are known as limiting amino acids.

Measuring the Protein in Food

Foods can be chemically analysed to give the crude protein percentage which is the value you see written on bags of compound feeds. This value is only a guideline as it gives you no idea of how digestible that protein is, nor any guide to protein quality. Thus bran has a high crude protein value but low digestible crude protein value and has a poor balance of amino acids.

Fats and Oils

Fat is an important energy source, releasing two-and-a-quarter times the energy of carbohydrate on a weight for weight basis. It also acts as a protective layer under the skin and around the internal organs, and is essential for good skin and coat condition.

Fats are made up of chains of fatty acids which are broken down in the small intestine and absorbed across the gut wall. Traditionally horses have received low levels of fat in the diet: only 2 to 3% compared with a human intake of over 50%! However, it may be beneficial to the performance horse to increase the oil level in the ration so that more energy can be supplied without increasing the value of the feed or feeding too many 'heating' ingredients. Feeding a teacup full of oil a day during hot, dry weather will help stop your horse's feet becoming brittle.

Water

Water is involved in nearly all of the chemical reactions that keep the body alive. About 60% of an adult horse is actually water — hard to believe when he treads on you! Adequate water provision is essential in the performance horse as a sweating horse can become seriously ill due to dehydration.

Minerals and Vitamins

The performance horse is kept stabled with only limited access to grazing and is fed a variety of conserved, processed and heat-treated foods. Inevitably the mineral and vitamin levels of these foods will have suffered by these treatments and the horse's ability to synthesise water-soluble vitamins in the gut will be upset by rapid dietary changes and stress. Consequently a mineral and vitamin supplement should be used if a traditional hay, oats and bran ration is fed. However, if a good quality compound feedstuff is used as specified by the manufacturer, a supplement should not be necessary.

Rationing

A ration of a performance horse is decided after three important factors have been assessed:

- size
- condition
- work

Size

The amount of food a horse needs to keep him alive and to maintain his body weight is called the *maintenance requirement*. It is determined by his weight: common sense tells you that a big horse eats more than a little one! Horses will eat about 2.5% of their body weight a day. Thus a 500 kg (1100 lb) horse, a 16.1 hh middleweight, will eat 12.5 kg (31 lb) of food a day. One very important aspect of a ration is that it satisfies the horse's energy requirements without exceeding his appetite.

Condition

A horse in poor condition will need more food than one in good or overweight condition.

Condition scoring

The condition of your horse should be monitored regularly and used as part of his profile. Condition can be measured using a scoring system from 0 to 5 which assesses the weight displacement along the neck and over the back, ribs and quarters (Fig. 6.3).

0: Starvation. Croup and hip bones sharp and prominent. Cut-up behind. Spinous processes of back vertebrae prominent. Ribs showing and ribcage prominent.

$\frac{1}{2}$: As above but less obvious.

1: Still thin but a little more muscle definition.

$1\frac{1}{2}$: Bones beginning to lose their sharpness; front half of ribcage covered but back half still defined.

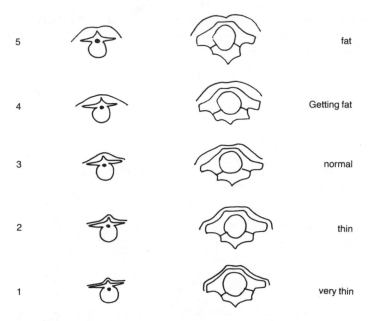

Fig. 6.3 Condition scoring — assessment of the weight displacement over back and hind quarters.

2: *Approaching normal.* Withers, croup and hip bones still well defined but less easy to feel. NB Hunters and some eventers may look like this.

$2\frac{1}{2}$: *Normal.* Hip bones and spinous processes defined but not prominent, well covered with muscle; adequate subcutaneous fat. Ribcage covered and last three ribs felt with slight pressure. Muscles well defined. What you are aiming for!

3: *Getting fat*: Bones becoming more difficult to feel.

$3\frac{1}{2}$: *Fat*: Neck cresty; cannot see last three ribs; definition of bones lost.

4: *Obese*: Large masses of fat carried on neck, quarters and back. Can only feel ribs on pressure. Deep pressure needed to feel croup and hip bones.

5: *Excessively obese*: spine makes a hollow; pads of fat on shoulders and quarters; impossible to feel ribs, croup or hips. NB Laminitic.

Skin and coat condition

The coat should be glossy to look at, and also feel smooth and silky. The skin should be loose and pliable, and when picked up in a pinch and released should return smoothly and easily to its former position

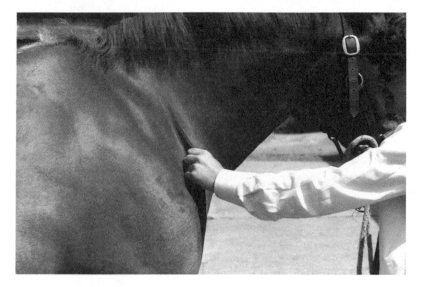

Fig. 6.4 Skin pinch test.

(Fig. 6.4). Any delay indicates either a degree of dehydration or a lack of subcutaneous fat.

Blood testing

Sub-clinical illness which causes below-par performance can only be identified through blood testing. The problem may be worms, bacterial or viral infection, dehydration or anaemia. Occasionally a change in diet can be all that is needed, or it may be a job for the vet. However, a blood test every 4 to 6 months can be an invaluable addition to your horse's profile.

Teeth

A tooth problem can cause your horse to be difficult to ride and to lose condition. Imagine trying to eat or accept the bit with your tongue and cheeks being lacerated at every chew! Teeth should be checked and rasped regularly: at least twice a year and as often as every 6 weeks if the horse has a problem.

Table 6.1 is designed to give you a guide to producing rations for your performance horse assuming that he weighs about 500 kg: a 16.1 hh light- to middleweight. Obviously all horses are individuals, and this guide as based on the mythical 'average' horse.

The ration is very simplistic as it includes only hay and one concentrate; providing adequate energy and protein are fed, a combination

Table 6.1 Ration fed to 500 kg 16.1 hh horse in various stages of work.

Work level	Digestible energy required per kg (MJ)	Crude protein required (%)	Ratio Hay: concentrates	Ration Hay 8 MJ DE/kg (lbs in brackets)	Ration Concentrate (lbs in brackets)	Feed
Maintenance	9	8.5	90:10	7½ (16½)	1 (2¼)	Horse and pony cubes (10 MJ DE/kg)
Light (getting fit)	9.5	8.5	80:20	7½ (16½)	2 (4½)	Horse and pony cubes
Light to medium (novice horse trials)	10	9	70:30	6½ (14)	3½ (8)	Event cubes (11 MJ DE/kg)
Medium (intermediate horse trials)	11	9.5	60:40	6½ (14)	5 (11)	Event cubes
Hard (advanced horse trials)	12	10	40:60	5½ (12)	6½ (14)	Oats (14 MJ DE/kg) + protein conc
Fast (racing)	13½	11	30:70	3½ (7½)	8½ (18)	Oats + protein concentrate

Note: Salt, limestone and cod liver oil should also be fed. If oats are fed, a supplement should be added to the ration.

of cereals can be given. By using Table 6.2 showing nutritive values, check that you are not over- or underfeeding. For example, 1 kg of oats (14 MJ DE per kg) will replace 1.5 kg of horse and pony cubes.

Practical feeding

The Rules of Feeding

These rules have evolved over many years and, even though our scientific knowledge of nutrition has vastly increased, as far as practical feeding is concerned they still hold good.

- In order to keep your horse healthy and to keep your feed bills under control, remember: *feed little and often*. The horse is a trickle feeder with a small stomach and a digestive system designed to receive small, high-fibre feeds frequently. A 4 lb (1.8 kg) feed or one that fills two-thirds of a stable bucket is adequate; bigger feeds are wasteful.
- *Make all dietary changes gradually*. The types of bugs in the gut depend on the horse's diet. Change the diet suddenly and some bacteria will be starved and die, releasing toxins which may cause colic or laminitis.
- *Feed plenty of roughage*. The horse is designed to eat grass: reduce the roughage intake below 25% and gut function will be disturbed.
- *Do not work fast immediately after feeding*. The stomach lies directly under the lungs, and a full stomach will prevent them from functioning properly. Exercise also causes the hormone adrenaline to be released; blood is diverted from the gut to the muscles and digestion is inhibited.
- *Stick to a feeding routine*. The horse is a creature of habit and responds to familiar and regular routines.
- *Maximum time between feeds*. Mobility of the gut will decrease if left without food for any considerable length of time. The horse should not be left without food for more than 8 hours.
- *Feeding when travelling long distances*. Water should be offered frequently on long journeys. Journeys of over 8 hours' duration should be broken and the horse offered a small feed. Horses that are upset by travelling and therefore sweat should be fed electrolytes.

Reduced Appetite

A horse that is not eating is trying to tell you something. Absence of appetite may be a sign of disease, injury or metabolic dysfunction. If your horse is healthy check for:

Table 6.2 Nutritive values of some feedstuffs fed to horses.

	DE (MJ/KG)	CP (%)	Oil (%)	Ca (g/kg)	P (g/kg)	Notes
Good grass hay	8.0	8.0	2.7	2.9	1.7	
Poor grass hay	7.0	4.0	2.0	2.9	1.7	Low protein
Alfalfa hay	7.6	15	1.7	11.4	1.9	High protein and calcium
Big bale silage	9.2	10.0	3.5	5.3	2.6	Good energy and protein
Oats	14.0	9.6	4.5	0.7	3.0	
Barley	16.0	9.5	1.8	0.6	3.3	
Maize	17.0	8.5	3.8	0.2	3.0	High energy
Bran	10.0	15.5	3.0	1.0	12.1	Very high phosphorus
Sugar beet pulp	14.0	7.0	1.0	10.0	11.0	
Horse and pony cubes	10.0	10.0	3.0	0.85	0.5	
Event cubes	11.0	11.5	3.25	0.85	0.5	
Racehorse cubes	13.0	14.5	3.25	0.85	0.5	

- stale food in mangers
- poor quality feed
- changes in a compound feed
- overwork
- overfeeding
- teeth problems

Routine Care of the Equine Athlete

Fitness

No matter how perfect our horse is, it requires correct feeding, training and fitness for him to realise his full athletic potential. Regardless of the eventual competitive goal, getting a horse fit can be divided into four phases:

- preliminary work
- development work
- fast work
- maintaining fitness

Preliminary work

The thoroughness of the preliminary work is of vital importance to the success of your fittening programme. Think of a pyramid: the broader the base the higher the peak that can be safely reached. When labour was cheap and one lad did one horse, hunters walked for 4 weeks, working up to 2 hours every morning and 1 hour in the afternoons. However, times have changed! Nevertheless all horses should be given a minimum of 2 weeks' walking work, starting at 20 minutes on day 1 and working up to 60 minutes by the end of the first week.

During the second week the horse should walk actively in a good outline for up to 2 hours. Unfortunately many of us have full-time jobs and can only ride our horse for 90 minutes a day. If this is so, walk for $2\frac{1}{2}$ to 3 weeks. During week 3, short periods of trot can be introduced, gradually building up until, by the end of week 4, 15 to 20 minutes of a 90-minute hack is trotting. Try to utilise hills to reduce the jarring that road-trotting inflicts, and never trot fast but make sure that the horse is active and in a correct outline. The purpose of this period is to accustom the horse to carrying weight and to gradually tone up tendons, muscles, ligaments and bone. The horse should not sweat and blow; if he does, reduce the trotting and extend the walking period.

Development work

By the end of the fourth week of road work, with some uphill trotting towards the end of the period, the horse should be ready to go to the next stage of training. Development training will vary depending on which sport the horse is being prepared for: the polo pony will be given some basic schooling and stick-and-ball work; the showjumper will start gymnastic jumping; the racehorse will be cantering; the long-distance horse will step up speed and distance; and the event horse will be given suppling exercises on the flat and over small fences.

Whatever the type of horse, canter work should be slow and short initially and should be increased gradually so that, by the end of the sixth week, three or four periods of steady cantering can be included in the exercise programme. If interval training is to be used, it can be introduced during week 6; three 3-minute canters at 350 mpm would be a good starting point. At the end of each workout the horse will be blowing, but this should not be excessive and the horse should recover quickly. Canter work should be gradually built up until, by the end of week 7, the horse is ready to do some fast work. In interval training the horse should be doing three 4-minute canters at 400 mpm twice a week. Remember that most horses will also do a considerable amount of cantering during the other days of the week, whether flat or jump schooling.

Fast work

By now the horse should be well developed in terms of muscle, bone, tendons and ligaments, but we have been careful not to make the horse blow and sweat excessively. It is time to stress the respiratory system by introducing short periods of gallop. Some horses may never need to do fast work; dressage horses and showjumpers continue development work but at a more advanced level.

By week 12 the novice one-day-event horse should be able to do three 5-minute canters at 400 mpm, the last minute of the last canter being slightly faster at 550 mpm. The point-to-pointer should canter 5 days a week and gallop during two of those sessions. A 5-furlong gallop (600 mpm) would be adequate if backed up by plenty of steady canter work.

Maintaining fitness

Once fit the horse should not need as much fast work and the routine can be varied to suit the individual horse. It will depend on how frequently and at what level it is working or competing. Try not to over-fitten your horse: it will not do him any good, mentally or physically. Do not be frightened to back off a horse and give him a couple of days off in the field if he has gone 'over the top'. He will be more relaxed and easier to ride!

7
The physiology of the equine athlete

In order to get the best performance from our horses we must not only understand how to develop correct musculature and ride him properly, we must also understand a little of how his body functions and responds to our demands. The body systems involved in performance include the digestive system — without correct feeding we will get nowhere; the circulatory system; the respiratory system; bones; tendons, ligaments and muscles; and, controlling the whole, the nervous system.

The Skeletal System

The skeletal system constitutes the framework of the horse, containing, protecting and supporting the other organs.

Bone — Its Growth and Development

Bone is made up of a small number of cells embedded in a matrix which is produced and maintained by these cells. Cells called osteoblasts encourage collagen fibres to become mineralised, mainly by calcium and phosphorus, to become bone. This process continues throughout the animal's life because the skeleton is able to respond to the challenge of load-bearing, and disuse actually causes bone mass to decrease. Hence strong, functional bones are only maintained by being used and stressed in a controlled manner. Bone can only grow or adapt by the addition or removal of tissue at one of its existing surfaces; in other words it cannot grow from the inside out. In order for bones to grow or strengthen, there has to be carefully coordinated activity of bone-building cells (osteoblasts) and bone-destroying cells (osteoclasts). This coordination is seen most clearly at the *growth plates*. All bones start in the embryo as cartilage which is invaded by osteoblasts which then lay down bone. By the time the foal is born all that remains of the cartilage in the long bones, for example the cannon bone, are horizontal plates of cartilage lying between the shaft and the end of the bone, known as the *epiphyses* or *growth plates* (Fig. 7.1). Long bones increase in length by proliferation of the cartilage within the growth

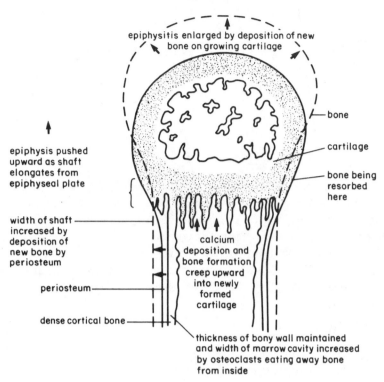

epiphysitis enlarged by deposition of new
bone on growing cartilage

epiphysis pushed
upward as shaft
elongates from
epiphyseal plate

bone

cartilage

bone being
resorbed
here

width of shaft
increased by
deposition of
new bone by
periosteum

calcium
deposition and
bone formation
creep upward
into newly
formed
cartilage

periosteum

dense cortical bone

thickness of bony wall maintained
and width of marrow cavity increased
by osteoclasts eating away bone
from inside

Fig. 7.1 The activity of the epiphyseal plate.

plate and its continuing replacement by bone. Once that bone has
reached its mature size the growth plate is invaded and replaced by
bone, and bone stops growing. Disruption of the growth plates is seen
as *epiphysitis* in fast-growing young horses. The new bone which is laid
down at the growth plate is modelled and remodelled so that the width
and thickness of the bone keep pace with the increase in length.

Correct training will give the horse maximum skeletal strength. By
loading the bone with daily periods of suitable exercise it is protected
from reabsorption and provided with the stimulus to lay down new
bone. This adaptive response will be enhanced by the type of strain put
on the bone, not just the size of the strain. Changes will also cause the
bone to adapt, thus turning and accelerating are important. Effectively
a horse's bone mass reflects the vigour, diversity and level of his activity. The daily duration of his work may not be as important as strain
quickly perceived and acted upon. In practical terms a horse's bone
strength will be maximised by giving him a small amount of vigorous
activity accompanied by a variety of movements placing different types
of stress on the bone, e.g. gymnastic jumping and lateral work.

Before we leave the subject of bone, we must also think of its growth and development. Bone needs exercise to stimulate growth because exercise stimulates the good circulation which is necessary to provide a good supply of blood, which carries the nutrition for growth, repair and increased development and removes waste products.

Young horses that are bred as future athletes must be given adequate exercise for proper development. Although it is not always practical, there is great value in running young horses in large areas in the herd situation. An old farmer friend of one of the authors had a wonderful arrangement and produced some very fine animals. He had a large farm with other stock. The horses (yearlings and two-, three- and four-year-olds) ran together in about 25 acres with water at one end and the daily feed at the other. The land was undulating, and to get to the food these horses had to negotiate ditches, large logs, lots of little combinations of obstacles, sharp turns and banks. This 'gymnasium' was purpose built, and the design was such that after the horses had finished eating they could amble through the field back to the pasture without having to go through the gymnasium again. One would think that problems would arise from the activities in the 'gymnasium' area, but surprisingly these horses seemed to have a good survival instinct and learned to be careful. When they came in to be broken, they were fit, tough and mature mentally. These horses had good, strong 'top outlines', which were well developed before they were asked to carry the weight of the rider. They were already athletes in training, and customers came from outside the UK, particularly from Ireland, to buy them.

Bone moulding or bone remodelling takes place in young horses and children. It is for this reason that training children as gymnasts and dancers is begun very early in life before the bones have finished growing. The training exercises influence the bone to grow in the way which gives the most advantage to the body to accommodate the work imposed upon it. Good circulation is stimulated by these activities, and growth and bone moulding take place.

Of course bone growth can be influenced to develop in a way that will not benefit the body, for example from hours of bad posture. Such posture can cause the body many problems that usually manifest later in life.

If young horses are given the right sort of exercise and the necessary food, their bodies will become better prepared for their future work. When we refer to exercise, we do not mean lungeing or ridden work. Lungeing very young horses can itself cause trouble. If this is the only way they can be exercised, then it is best left to an expert who appreciates the potential dangers and who can programme the work accordingly.

The Muscular System

Attached to the skeleton are tendons, ligaments and muscles which coordinate to move the bone and hence the horse. There are several types of muscle in the horse's body, smooth muscle in the organs of the gut and reproductive system, cardiac muscle in the heart, and skeletal muscle which is responsible for locomotion. Skeletal muscle is made up of cigar-shaped cells varying in length from several millimetres to over 30 cm. These cells are bound together in bundles, several of which are held together by connective tissue to give a structure more familiar as a Sunday leg of lamb (Fig. 2.12)! Muscle cells are made up of microscopic myofibrils which are contractile proteins. When stimulated by a nerve impulse, these proteins slide over one another in such a way as to shorten the muscle fibre length. Hence the entire muscle contracts. Surrounding the myofibrils are large amounts of a special substance called myoglobin which stores and transports oxygen and glycogen. Glycogen is stored glucose which can be rapidly mobilised and used in conjunction with the oxygen to produce energy in the form of ATP (adenosine triphosphate), which is then used for muscle contraction.

Muscle Fibre Types

Several different types of muscle fibre have been identified in both horses and humans. These fall into two main categories, slow twitch and fast twitch fibres. Broadly speaking the slow twitch fibres are equivalent to the dark leg meat on a Christmas turkey; they are specialised for endurance activity, e.g. standing up! These fibres do not generate a lot of power but contract, slowly and steadily, for long periods of time using oxygen very efficiently. Fast twitch fibres are equivalent to the breast meat of a turkey: they are capable of generating the large amount of short-term power necessary for launching a turkey into the air! On closer examination it has been found that these fast twitch fibres also fall into two main categories, fast twitch high oxidative (FTH) and fast twitch low oxidative (FTL) fibres. FTL fibres although very powerful can only work effectively for short periods of time because they work anaerobically — without oxygen — which results in a build-up of lactic acid. Lactic acid causes fatigue and prevents the fibres contracting. On the other hand FTH fibres can use oxygen quite efficiently while still generating a good deal of power. Thus FTL fibres would be utilised by a racehorse jumping from the stalls, by an eventer for the explosion of power needed when jumping or by the sprinter throughout its race. FTH fibres are used by the speed and endurance horse, e.g. the eventer and a National Hunt horse galloping between fences.

Changes with Training

As a horse muscles up, individual muscles become bigger due to increased muscle cell diameter. Large muscles can generate more instant power as in the human weight lifter, the dressage horse or, that ultimate sprinter, the quarter horse. Power may not be the only objective. Endurance is often important, so when training the eventer the regime aims to increase the oxygen-using capacity of the fast twitch fibres. This enables the horse to travel at speed for prolonged periods without the build-up of fatigue and of lactic acid. Increased aerobic capacity is also associated with more glycogen in the muscles for energy production and better utilisation of dietary fat. In order for these changes to take place, the correct stimuli must be given.

The Cardiovascular System

In order to produce energy aerobically, oxygen must be delivered to the muscles swiftly and efficiently via the blood which is pumped by the heart through the arteries to the tiny capillaries that supply the muscle fibres. The heart consists of two muscular pumps joined together, the right and left ventricles (Fig. 7.2). Blood is collected by the veins, having released its oxygen to the tissues, and is returned to the right atrium. This small collecting chamber contracts to force blood into the right ventricle which contracts to send blood to the lungs to collect oxygen. Simultaneously, oxygenated blood returns to the heart from the lungs via the pulmonary vein and is collected in the left atrium which contracts and pushes the blood into the left ventricle which in turn pushes blood out of the aorta and round the rest of the body to deliver its load of oxygen (Fig. 7.3). The right ventricle has thinner walls than the left ventricle, which has to push blood through the arteries at high pressure so that it reaches all parts of the body. The arteries are elastic to cope with and maintain this high pressure. As the blood passes through the small arteries (arterioles) and capillaries, the blood pressure rapidly drops to 60% of aorta pressure. Eventually the red blood cells have to move through these tiny tubes in single file and may even have to become misshapen to squeeze through. The walls of the blood vessels are permeable to nutrients and oxygen carried in the blood, enabling these to pass through to nourish the tissue and produce energy.

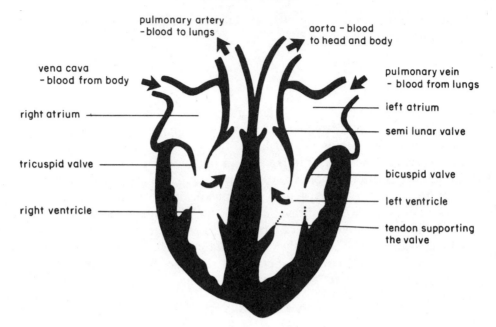

Fig. 7.2 The heart.

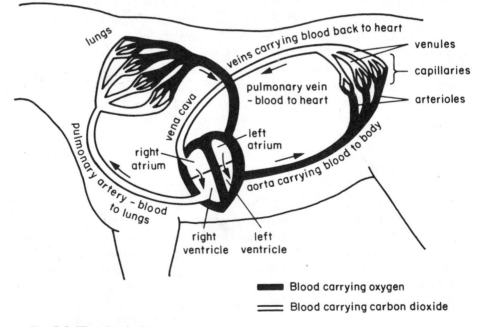

Fig. 7.3 The circulation.

The amount of blood distributed through the tissues varies when the horse is resting and exercising. At rest it is distributed as follows:

Organ	% Blood
Brain	5
Kidneys	13
Gut	26
Skeletal muscle	13
Spleen	30

On exercise the blood supply to the muscles increases dramatically to about 88%, showing the importance of getting nutrients and oxygen to the exercising muscles. Oxygen uptake can increase by 50 times due to

- increased blood to muscles
- increased heart rate
- release of red blood cells stored in the spleen

The Effects of Exercise

These can be summarised as follows:

- increased heart rate
- increased cardiac output
- stimulation of heart muscle
- increased flow of blood through the lungs
- increased respiration rate
- more blood to muscle
- more blood to skin for heat loss

The horse's resting heart rate is on average 36 to 40 beats per minute and in a fit horse may be as low as 26 beats per minute. The heart rate may rise as high as 240 beats per minute during strenuous exercise. As exercise starts, the heart rate rises rapidly and peaks 30–35 seconds later. It may then drop to a steady rate during steady exercise. Any further increases in heart rate, e.g. with prolonged exercise or increased effort, tend to be more gradual. After the horse stops exercising, the heart rate drops most rapidly in the first 2 minutes and then recovers more gradually. The time taken for the heart rate to return to normal resting values depends on the duration and intensity of the exercise, the horse's fitness and the environment (heat and humidity).

The Blood

Blood is the transport system of the body and must be healthy and efficient for top athletic performance. It makes up about 10% of the horse's body weight. Thus a 500 kg horse would have about 50 litres (11 gallons) of blood. In the resting horse about 20% of this blood is in the pulmonary circulation (i.e. in the lungs and associated blood vessels), 15% in the heart and arteries, 30% in the veins, and 30% in the spleen. The spleen acts as a storage organ of red blood cells which are 'resting' while the horse is at rest.

Exercise and Training

On exercise the horse's demand for oxygen increases, and, in response to this, adrenaline causes the spleen to release its stored red blood cells thus increasing the oxygen carrying capacity of the blood. The body also responds by producing more red blood cells so that the horse's resting packed cell volume (PCV) may increase by 15%. (The PCV is a measurement of the proportion of the blood that is solid, i.e. that consists of red and white blood cells. Normally this value is in the region of 40%.) Thus blood volume, haemoglobin concentration and oxygen carrying capacity can all increase with training.

Exercise can also cause adverse changes in the blood. If the horse cannot breathe fast enough to expel all the carbon dioxide which is a byproduct of energy production, the blood becomes too acid, a condition called respiratory acidosis. Metabolic acidosis occurs when lactic acid, the byproduct of anaerobic muscle contraction, accumulates in the blood over several days.

Echinocytosis

A blood disorder has been identified involving abnormally shaped red blood cells called echinocytes. Normally a red blood cell is a characteristic bioconcave disc whereas echinocytes are spherical with well defined spine-like spicules. This appears to be a membrane fault spontaneously acquired in the spleen which impedes capillary blood flow and consequently reduces oxygen supply to the muscles. It means that the horse cannot work efficiently, which increases the risk of significant injury when the horse is working hard, and may be associated with exercise-induced pulmonary haemorrhage (bleeding) and azoturia.

The Respiratory System

The respiratory system consists of the airways of the head and neck (Fig. 7.4) and the lungs (Fig. 7.5). It has several functions including:

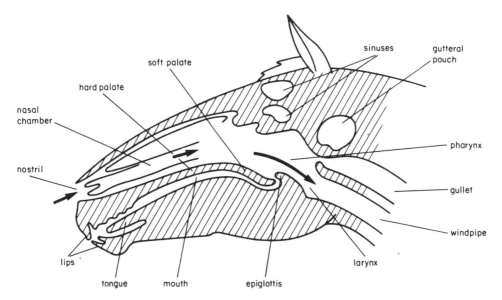

Fig. 7.4 The airways of the head and neck.

(1) humidification and warming of inhaled air
(2) providing a defence against contaminants in the atmosphere
(3) acting as a reservoir of blood for the heart
(4) enabling gas exchange

In other words the task of the respiratory system is to get air containing oxygen into the depths of the lungs, making the air warm and moist along the way, extracting large particles of dust, and eventually swapping the oxygen in the air for the carbon dioxide produced in the tissues.

The airways that conduct air into the lungs are the nasal cavity, nasopharynx, larynx, trachea (windpipe), bronchi and bronchioles. The main body of the lung consists of tiny blind-ended sacs called alveoli. It is estimated that the human lung contains a quarter of a billion alveoli, each of which is supplied by around a thousand tiny blood capillaries. This means that there is a huge surface area for oxygen exchange so that each breath the horse takes results in a maximum amount of oxygen being extracted from the air and passed into the bloodstream across the thin alveolus wall. The size of the horse's lungs is related to his body weight and is larger relative to most other species. At rest a 500 kg horse would breathe in and out 5 to 7 litres (tidal volume) of air whereas when galloping he would breathe in up to 42 litres.

Breathing is affected by the muscles of the diaphragm, external intercostals and abdominal muscles. As the horse breathes in, the

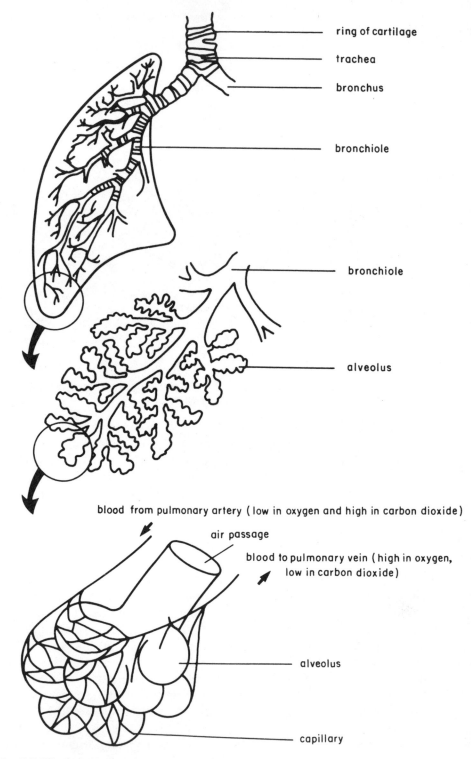

ring of cartilage

trachea

bronchus

bronchiole

bronchiole

alveolus

blood from pulmonary artery (low in oxygen and high in carbon dioxide)

air passage

blood to pulmonary vein (high in oxygen, low in carbon dioxide)

alveolus

capillary

Fig. 7.5 The lungs.

intercostals contract to move the ribcage upwards and out. Simultaneously the dome-shaped diaphragm contracts and flattens. These effects result in the volume of the chest becoming greater, and air rushes in to fill up the lungs. Breathing out at rest is mainly accomplished by recoil of the elastic lungs and chest wall, but when the horse is exerting itself this recoil does not empty the lungs sufficiently and the abdominal muscles contract to squeeze more air out so that more, new, air can enter.

Respiration rate, how many breaths the horse takes per minute, is governed by the oxygen demands of the body and by the stride frequency when the horse is galloping. Movements of the gut (the visceral piston) and the head and neck (the cranio-cervical pendulum) dictate whether the horse breathes in or out, as shown in Fig. 2.22. As the horse gallops, there is a moment of suspension when the head moves up and the gut is pulled back allowing air to rush into the lungs. When the horse lands, its head moves down and the gut moves forward, compressing the lungs and aiding exhalation or breathing out. Thus the horse's respiration rate cannot be more than about 180 when galloping. When a vet is listening to the horse's wind at the gallop, he watches for its front legs to hit the ground. He knows the horse is breathing out then, and any abnormal exhalatory noise can be identified.

Tissue Respiration

Breathing results in oxygen being taken from the air into the bloodstream and hence to the tissues. Once in the tissues it is used to produce energy by a process called tissue respiration. This energy can then be used for muscle contraction and movement of the horse. In order for a horse to produce energy, glucose is needed. This is extracted from the diet during digestion and is stored in the muscles and liver in a special storage form called glycogen. When the horse starts to work, the glycogen stores are mobilised as glucose.

The source of energy actually used for muscle contraction is a substance called adenosine triphosphate (ATP); ATP can be produced by breaking down glucose in either the presence or the absence of oxygen, that is, aerobically or anaerobically.

Aerobic respiration (Fig. 7.7)

This process takes place very efficiently in slow twitch and fast twitch high oxidative muscle fibres; 1 unit of glucose is 'burned up' in the presence of oxygen to form 36 units of ATP. The process is very efficient at producing energy, but the rate at which energy can be produced

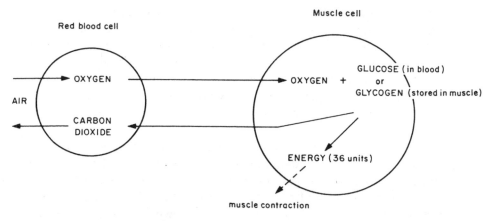

Fig. 7.6 Aerobic metabolism.

is limited by the rate at which oxygen can be transported to the tissue, which is influenced by many factors:

- respiration rate
- lung or alveolar volume
- blood supply to the lungs
- speed at which the blood is supplying the lungs, i.e. heart rate
- red blood cell number
- haemoglobin concentration

At very high or maximal levels of work the demand for energy exceeds the rate at which ATP can be produced aerobically and energy starts to be produced anaerobically.

Anaerobic respiration (Fig. 7.7)

This process takes place in the fast twitch low oxidative muscle fibres which are specially adapted to produce powerful effort for short periods of time. Glucose is broken down in the absence of oxygen to produce ATP. However, far less energy is produced: aerobic respiration is 12 times more efficient than anaerobic respiration. Also a poisonous by-product called lactic acid is produced, which is taken by the blood to the liver to be rendered harmless. However, if intense exercise continues, lactic acid accumulates in the muscles and appears to be a major contributor to fatigue and muscle cramps.

The production of energy can be summarised as shown in Table 7.1.

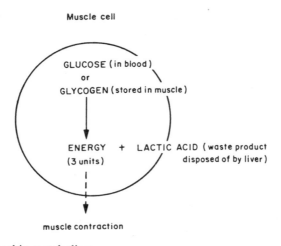

Fig. 7.7 Anaerobic metabolism.

Table 7.1 Production of energy during exercise.

	Aerobic Submaximal work	Anaerobic Maximal work
Heart rate (beats per minute)	<200	200–246
Speed	Walk, trot, canter	Gallop (500 mpm+)
Muscle fibres	Slow twitch	Fast twitch, low oxidative
	Fast twitch, high oxidative	
Duration of exercise	Long term	Short term
Contributors to fatigue	Glucose depletion	Lactic acid build-up

Aims of Training

Horses competing in different disciplines will have different types of energy-production requirement. The sprinting racehorse needs to be able to work anaerobically, producing large amounts of power for short periods, whereas the National Hunt horse and eventer must be able to sustain speed over longer distances, and the driving horse and endurance horse have to maintain slower speeds for long periods. Part of getting any horse fit other than a sprinter is to increase the body's ability to work aerobically and hence delay the onset of lactic acid build-up and fatigue as long as possible. To accomplish this the horse should be exposed in training to the types of stress encountered during competition. In order to avoid overstress, this exposure can be quite short: just enough to cause the body to adapt so that, when that stress is encountered again, the body recognises it and can cope. Thus the advanced three-day-event horse which is expected to gallop at 690 mpm over a steeplechase course of $1\frac{3}{4}$ miles (2415 or 2760 m) and jump round a cross-country course of $4\frac{1}{2}$ miles (5000–6200 m) at 570 mpm would be expected to work up to three 8-minute canters at the following speeds:

1×8 min   500 mpm ($2\frac{1}{2}$ miles (4 km)); 3 min walk
1×8 min   550 mpm; 3 min walk
1×8 min   500 mpm; last minute 690 mpm

Monitoring Fitness

Blood Tests

A horse's blood is made up of various components which are present in characteristic amounts. Each horse's blood test results should lie within a 'normal' range of values for these components. A vet can collect a sample of blood from the horse's jugular vein and have the results ready in a couple of days. The results can be compared with the normal values, and deviation can help the vet confirm a diagnosis of illness or assess the horse's wellbeing and fitness to compete. For a blood test to be of any use in determining any deviations from normal, that horse's normal values must be known. In other words you cannot say if the horse is ill unless you know his healthy blood profile.

Components of the Blood (Fig. 7.9)

(1) *Plasma*. This is a straw-coloured fluid which carries the cellular component of the blood. Plasma contains *fibrinogen*, which aids blood clotting, and *serum*, which carries dissolved nutrients and hormones.
(2) *Red blood cells*. These carry oxygen to the tissues and return carbon dioxide to the lungs.
(3) *White blood cells*. There are five types of white blood cell or leucocyte: neutrophils, basophils, lymphocytes, monocytes and eosinophils. They are concerned with fighting disease and infection and are a vital part of the body's immune system.

Blood Collection

The skin, usually over the jugular vein, is swabbed with surgical spirit and a needle is inserted into the vein; 2 to 3 ml of blood is removed and mixed immediately with an anticoagulant to prevent clotting. A further 5 to 7 ml is taken, placed in a separate tube and allowed to clot for serum examination.

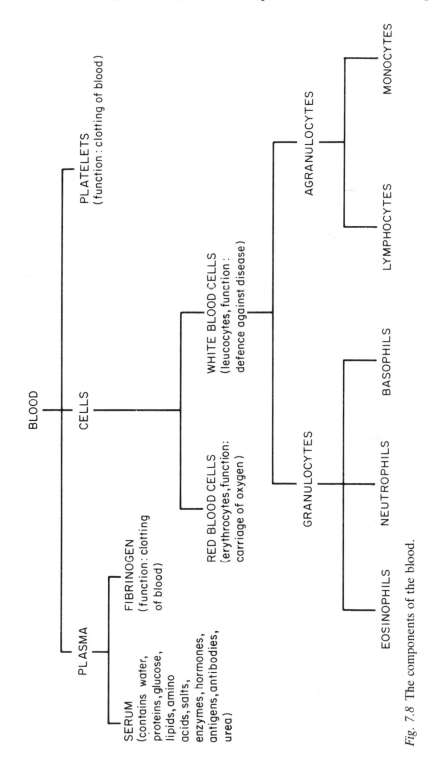

Fig. 7.8 The components of the blood.

Few horses appear to resent this procedure — much less so than an injection of antibiotic. It is important that the horse is upset as little as possible and that it has not been exercised that day as some values change after stress and exercise. The sample should reach the laboratory within 24 hours of collection because blood deteriorates if kept too long.

Blood Analysis

The unclotted blood is placed in special microscope slides with counting chambers, and the total red cells are counted by means of sophisticated electronic equipment. The haemoglobin content of the blood is estimated. Unclotted blood is then spun at high speed (centrifuged) so that the cells all pack in one end of a parallel-sided tube. By measuring the length of the cells in the tube, the PCV percentage is calculated. This test indicates that a horse is dehydrated if there is a larger than normal PCV. Along with red cell count and haemoglobin concentration, PCV can be used to calculate the mean corpuscular haemoglobin concentration (MCHC). These tests can indicate anaemia due to deficiencies of iron, folate or vitamin B_{12}.

A white cell count is also carried out. Any deviation from the normal numbers of white cells is usually because a greater demand is being made upon them. For example, increased neutrophil numbers indicate bacterial infection and/or inflammation. Lymphocytes produce antibodies to specific diseases and germs; those that react to viruses are different and can be seen in a blood film, often before the illness is detectable. Eosinophils multiply in allergies (an allergy is an intolerance to foreign protein); eosinophil numbers also increase if the horse is suffering from a worm burden. Monocytes can increase as part of an immune reaction, or when bacterial infection is present, or if there is an internal parasite infection. White cells are counted as a whole and the different types are also counted.

Serum Examination

When blood is allowed to clot, the remaining fluid is called serum. When anticlotting agents are added and the cells are removed, the remaining fluid is called plasma. Plasma consists of serum plus the agents involved in clotting. Serum is examined for proteins and enzymes (biological catalysts that enable metabolic processes to take place), a process called serum biochemistry.

Serum proteins are of two main types: *albumin* and many *globulins*. Albumin is made in the liver when the diet is adequate, and globulins are produced by the immune system and are known as antibodies to disease. As the animal ages, more diseases are encountered; antibodies increase and so globulins and the total blood protein increases. Younger animals naturally have lower total protein in the blood, and this cannot be increased by feeding more protein. Low albumin usually indicates that the diet is poor or that albumin is being lost, as during worm infestation.

Correct functioning of organs of the body can be tested. For example, liver function is checked by protein estimations and serum protein and serum urea. Muscle is rich in an enzyme called creatine phosphokinase (CPK), the level of which increases in response to damage to muscle. Testing for this enzyme helps in diagnosis and treatment of azoturia.

With specialised equipment the blood can also be tested for a full range of minerals. It may be wise to have a horse's blood tested for selenium if you live in a selenium-deficient area.

It must be remembered that each horse is different: what is normal for one horse may be unusual for another. Ideally, not only should the normal for each horse be known but the results of the test should be compared with a table of the laboratory's normal range of results (Table 7.2).

Interpretation of the Blood Test

This is the job of the veterinary surgeon as it requires experience and professional expertise. However, some signs can be looked for:

Table 7.2 Normal range of blood test values.

Haematology	
Red cell count	8.5–11 million/mm
Haemoglobin concentration	13–17 g/100 ml
Packed cell volume	34–44%
Mean corpuscular volume	38–45 femtolitres
Mean corpuscular haemoglobin concentration	32–39 g/100 ml
White cells	6000–12 000/mm
Neutrophils	2000–8000/mm
Lymphocytes	1500–4000/mm
Eosinophils	100–600/mm
Monocytes	100–600/mm
Basophils	20–50/mm
Biochemistry	
Serum proteins	
total	55–75 g/litre
albumin	25–41 g/litre ⎱ 1:1 ratio
globulins	25–41 g/litre ⎰
Urea	20–45 mg/100 ml
CPK	20–80 Iu*/litre

*Iu = International unit.

(1) *Infection*
   (a) Bacterial
       * increased total white cell count
       * an increased percentage of neutrophils
   (b) Viral
       * increased total white cell count
       * more lymphocytes
       * presence of virus lymphocytes
(2) *Anaemia*
    True anaemia is rare in horses but may follow a viral infection
    or blood loss. Anaemia is diagnosed following a blood test
    which shows:
    * reduced red cell count
    * low haemoglobin concentration
    Anaemia is usually found in the following circumstances:
    * poor nutrition
    * worm burden
    * deficiencies of iron, vitamin B_{12}, folic acid
(3) *Dehydration*. This is a lack of body fluid caused by fluid loss
    being greater than fluid intake (e.g. after illness, exertion,
    water deprivation), and is shown by the PCV.
(4) *Muscle damage*. This may result from injury, exertion (espec-
    ially during dehydration or illness) or azoturia, and is shown by
    high CPK levels.

Monitoring Temperature, Pulse and Respiration

Temperature, pulse and respiration rates can be used to assess both
health and fitness. Taking these three simple measurements should be
incorporated into the daily routine of all conscientious horsemen. It
takes about the same amount of time as picking out feet, and is equally
important! You should know your horse's normal temperature, pulse
and respiration (TPR) so that if any deviations occur you know how
serious they are. For example, you suspect your horse has a viral
infection, so you take his temperature and it is 39°C — only 1°C above
normal — and so there may be nothing to worry about. However, your
horse's 'normal' may be 37°C, meaning that he has a fever of 2°C — a
more serious proposition. The horse's temperature will also be an
indication of how much work he has done, and is used as a measure of
whether or not he is fit to continue. For example, if the weather is hot
and humid, a horse's temperature will be taken in the 10-minute box
before the start of the cross-country phase. Any horse with a temperature of more than 40°C (103°F) at the end of the break would not be
allowed to continue.

The Pulse Rate

The pulse rate can be used in training programmes to ensure that the work given stresses the horse enough to increase his fitness without overstressing him. Used in conjunction with interval training, heart rate monitoring can help the horse with minimum stress. For example, the horse should be encouraged to work anaerobically for short periods of time in order to get to peak fitness. Once the horse's heart rate goes over 200 beats per minute it is working anaerobically. The speed at which the heart rate returns to normal after exercise (recovery rate) is an excellent indicator of fitness. One minute after work has stopped, the heart rate should be about 120 beats per minute if beneficial stress has occurred. If the heart rate is higher than this, the horse has worked too hard; if less than this, he has not worked hard enough.

The horse's heart rate will also go up if he is in pain or has a fever. Higher than normal rates during a workout may indicate that the horse is not his normal self and care should be taken: perhaps there is a slight problem that may be a lameness tomorrow if you work the horse today.

Pulse rate is taken where an artery passes over a bone. The artery on the cheekbone is used most commonly. A stethoscope can be used to listen directly to the heart on the left side of the horse just in front of the girth about a hand's breadth from the base of the chest. Sophisticated heart rate monitors that give a readout to the rider are available. These usually have electrodes that fit under the girth and saddle and connect to a digital readout which attaches to the rider's wrist or thigh and is easily read by the rider. Heart rate monitors although expensive are invaluable to the rider who is trying to get a horse to an advanced level of fitness for the first time. It is very hard to get the workout at the correct level if you have never ridden at that level before. The heart rate monitor can take out the guesswork so that you know when your horse is working anaerobically, and you can consequently develop the right feel for speeds for your horse.

Respiration Rate

Like the heart rate, respiration rate is an indication of health, fitness and stress. However, respiration rate is affected by environmental factors. In other words, if the weather is hot, the horse's respiration is higher than if the weather is cool. This means that respiration cannot be used accurately to monitor a horse's response to a training programme. It can be useful to observe the quality of a horse's breathing; a horse that is suffering from an allergy to hay or straw will probably have a higher breathing rate in the stable and the rate will increase more than expected during exercise and not recover to normal quickly.

In the absence of a stethoscope or heart rate monitor, the horse's breathing rate can be used during training to monitor the horse's response to the work you give him. However, remember that, on a hot, muggy day, the horse will not recover as well as on a cool, breezy day.

8
Care before, during and after competition exercise

Stable Management

The top-class athlete requires top-class management in all aspects of his life; an Olympic runner would not shut himself in his bedroom for 23 hours, inhaling dust and fungal spores, and then train intensively for 60 minutes a day! Aspects of stable management that require close attention are:

- stable design
- food
- bedding
- worming
- teeth
- grooming
- water provision

Stable Design and Bedding

The horse's environment should be as healthy as possible, with a large, airy, draught-free box. In order to protect the respiratory system from the adverse effects of the fungal spores found even in good quality hay and straw, it may be wise to feed soaked hay and bed on shavings as a matter of course. The human nose cannot detect the presence of spores, so get your hay tested or soak it for 12 hours to encourage the spores to swell so that they are eaten and not inhaled. An allergy may take several years to manifest itself as clinical signs such as coughing, but the horse may still be suffering to a minor degree and his lung capacity will be affected.

Worming

Stabled horses should still be wormed every 4 to 6 weeks. Remember that the redworm that your horse ingested during his holiday at grass will by now have produced larvae that are migrating through his body. Even though the droppings may show no evidence of worm eggs, immature larvae may still be present 12 months after the horse was initially infected.

Teeth

The horse has to have quite a severe tooth problem before he shows signs such as quidding and loss of condition. However, if a young horse carries his head on one side early in his training programme, sharp uncomfortable hooks can develop on the molars within 6 to 8 weeks. Some top riders have their horses' teeth examined several times a year to avoid bit evasion problems.

Grooming

Grooming is a very important routine and should include health checks such as taking the temperature and pulse and respiration rates. How can you judge and deviation from normal, indicating the onset of a viral disease for instance, if you don't know what 'normal' is? Some top trainers set great store in taking temperatures and will not 'work' horses, i.e. gallop or race them, if the temperature is as little as 0.5°C higher than normal. Thorough grooming also ensures that you are aware of all of your horse's normal lumps and bumps, know how hot his legs are in the morning and again in the evening, and know what condition his skin is in; a quick skin pinch test to assess dehydration is useful.

Water Provision

It is important to be aware of your horse's water drinking habits in the stable. Frequently horses are reluctant to drink away from home and during competitions. This can lead to severe problems if you are competing in hot, humid conditions. The more closely you can conform to your horse's preferred drinking habits, the more likely your horse is to drink when he is away from home. Don't just say, 'Oh, he never drinks away from home.' You could run into problems if you are away for several days.

Correct Warming up and Cooling down

Human athletes are meticulous with their warming up exercises. They are only too aware that, unless the body systems are correctly primed before work, the inevitable result is at best poor performance, at worst strains and sprains. The equine athlete should be treated the same way; the dressage horse should not be expected to go on the bit as soon as he comes out of the stable. You like to have a stretch and to wander about when you get out of bed, not go straight into press-ups! The type and degree of warm-up will obviously depend on the discipline, and are most important for the horse which is expected to produce speed. Racehorses are inadvertently warmed up quite well; initially they are walked round the paddock for up to 20 minutes and then cantered down to the start. They catch their breath while the girths are checked and are then ready for the off. Similarly the three-day-event horse is thoroughly warmed up by his roads and tracks before the cross-country phase. However, the one-day-event horse and hunter-trial horse is less likely to be so well prepared, and it is important that the rider is aware of this. The horse should have 10 minutes' walk and trot, a 3-minute canter and a 3-minute walk; having done this, if the start is delayed, a short canter immediately before starting will be sufficient.

Warming up ensures that sufficient blood is diverted from the core to the muscles that are going to be involved in locomotion. An inadequate blood supply will mean a shortage of nutrients (oxygen and glucose) for the contracting muscle, resulting in premature fatigue and subsequent injury. Warming up may require special attention to specific areas: athletes massage calf and thigh muscles prior to an event, and the same may be necessary for your horse.

Cooling down correctly is equally important. Look at the runner who has just finished a race and is hot and sweaty: he immediately puts on his track suit to prevent chilling and to keep his circulation going. Contrast this with the winning racehorse. He is pulled up and ridden to the winner's enclosure where he is untacked and a skimpy sweat sheet is put on. There he stands, blowing and sweating, until his jockey has weighed in and the result has been confirmed. There are several consequences arising from this treatment. The effect of cool air on the horse's sweating skin is to cause the peripheral blood vessels to constrict, making heat loss from the inside of the body difficult and yet chilling the outside of the horse. The fact that the horse is standing still results in blood being diverted away from the muscles as they no longer have a very high oxygen demand. This reduced blood supply may not be adequate to remove the lactic acid that has built up in the muscles during anaerobic tissue respiration. Pooling of lactic acid can lead to minor muscle damage that manifests itself as stiffness subsequent to exercise. We can go home and soak in a bath to help alleviate or partially prevent this stiffness. The horse cannot, and few equines have access to hot showers and infra-red lamps! Ideally horses should be cooled down at a slow trot until their pulse and respiration have returned to normal and they have stopped sweating. This amount of exercise keeps the blood circulating to the muscles and skin so that the lactic acid is dispersed and the horse cools down effectively.

Keeping the Horse Moving

Few grooms are dedicated enough to jog alongside their charges. A compromise is to walk the horse with a cooler rug on or a sweat sheet with a cotton sheet over the top; sweat sheets are not particularly effective unless they are covered by another layer. After 5 minutes' walking the horse can be untacked and the rugs replaced. If the saddle has been on for a very long time, it should be left on for longer than 5 minutes to allow the blood to return to the saddle area; sudden removal can cause pressure lumps and scalded backs.

Check Temperature, Pulse and Respiration

If the horse has been severely exerted, especially in hot humid conditions, the temperature, pulse and respiration should be taken to see how much above normal they are and to monitor how quickly they drop. These values are an indication of how severely stressed the horse is and how quickly it is recovering. The pulse can be taken, under the jaw or using a stethoscope, for 10 seconds, multiplying by six to get the pulse rate per minute. The temperature may be as much as 43°C (106°F). The type of breathing should be noted; a horse breathing deeply is taking in oxygen, and rapid, shallow breathing indicates that a horse is trying to cool down.

A fit horse should take no longer than 15 minutes for pulse and respiration rates to return to comfortable levels. The horse should be checked every 5 minutes until the values return to normal, which should be within an hour of completing exercise.

Washing down

The horse should be walked until the breathing has slowed to a comfortable rate — perhaps 15 minutes after an advanced three-day event — and then stood in a sheltered place. If the horse's temperature is no more than 41°C (104°F), tepid water will cool down the horse quite safely. The lower neck, inside the legs, the head and the belly should be sponged. The large muscle masses of the quarters and back should be avoided as sudden cooling may send these muscles into spasm. If the horse's temperature is between 41 and 43°C (104–106°F) and the weather is hot and humid, the horse must be cooled as quickly as possible to avoid heatstroke. The horse should be kept moving, and cold water and ice should be used on the horse in strategic places, e.g. under the tail, between the hind legs and on the head, where major arteries pass close to the skin. As the water evaporates from the horse's skin, it takes heat with it so the horse should be sponged again once it has dried until its temperature has returned to a safe level (40°C or 103°F). Sponging may have to be repeated several times. Remember that the horse must be kept moving so that the blood keeps circulating quickly.

Water Provision

The horse must not be given water until the temperature has dropped to 40°C (103°F) and the pulse and respiration have slowed. When a horse is exercising, blood is diverted from the gut to the muscle; while the horse is cooling, the blood needs to stay in the muscles. Drinking will cause the blood vessels that supply the stomach to expand, taking blood away from the muscles. The horse will not cool efficiently and may become colicky.

Once recovery is under way, and until the horse is completely cool, five swallows of water for every 50 m walked is adequate.

Checking for Injury

During untacking and sponging, the horse must be checked over for injury. Any found must be thoroughly cleaned and dressed with antibiotic cream or powder, but bandages should not be put on until the horse is cool. While the horse is being walked, it should be jogged for a few metres to check for soundness.

Once cool and dry the horse can be rugged up and its studs removed and feet picked out, and it can then be returned to its box to rest. The legs can now be poulticed or bandaged. Some people like to use a liniment and give the horse's legs a gentle rub down to aid circulation and ease tension; others use cooling clay poultices and gels. Any treatment should be covered by a stable bandage applied over thick padding. The bandage should not be tight, just firm enough to stay in place. There should be even pressure, and the bandage should give adequate support to the fetlock. The bandage provides warmth and support for a tired leg, and is there to control excess swelling should there be a slight injury which manifests itself overnight.

Keep Checking

The horse may break out in a sweat because although the skin and surface muscles are cool there may be heat and toxins deeper inside the muscles which the body needs to get rid of. The horse should be checked every 15 minutes for the next hour, looking for cold sweaty patches, restless behaviour, disturbed bedding, and reluctance to eat or drink. These signs could indicate the onset of azoturia or colic.

Signs of Overstress

The horse may show signs of overstress immediately after competition but these signs may not become apparent until the next day.

- Heat, swelling and pain will indicate injury in a specific area
- Reluctance to eat and listlessness may indicate pain, e.g. colic, azoturia, muscle injury
- Shaking indicates acute muscle fatigue; keep the horse warm and walk him in hand
- Until the horse is eating and drinking normally, he has not recovered: allow him plenty of rest; relaxing hacks and grazing in hand will also help.

Correct Feeding and Water Provision

The horse's ration should be so designed that it does not have to be changed during a competition. One of the rules of feeding states that changes to the ration should be made gradually to avoid digestive upset. As far as possible, feed the same ingredients in the same quantity at the same times before, during and after the competition. Inevitably there are a few exceptions!

Bulky Feeds and Water May Be Restricted Immediately prior to Fast Competition Work

A three-day-event horse would have its sugarbeet pulp reduced or omitted on the morning of its cross-country day, and either a small hay net or nothing depending on the start time. The water bucket should be removed one hour before start time.

A novice event horse could munch on its hay net while being plaited on the morning of his competition but should not receive any bulk while travelling until after the cross-country. Depending on your times, he may be able to have his lunch between dressage and showjumping providing that there is at least 2 hours' digestion time. He should be offered water at regular intervals during the day and allowed to wash his mouth out between the showjumping and cross-country even if they are very close together.

Long-distance horses should be encouraged to drink whenever water is available. Dehydration is a gradual process, and once the signs have been noticed you may have lost your competition! Horses that are reluctant to drink can be fed very sloppy sugarbeet pulp containing electrolytes.

After severe competition, or if the horse is very tired, feed the same ingredients as normal but in smaller quantities. Your horse will need a 'pick-me-up'. Try adding molasses or sugarbeet pulp: the sugar content will get energy into the system quickly.

Electrolytes should be added to the feed or water to compensate for those salts lost during sweating. Remember that a horse may still be sweating even if you don't see sweat dripping off it; it is just that the sweat is drying quickly. Electrolytes may have to be fed for several days if the horse worked hard and sweated heavily.

Do not overfeed a tired horse with concentrates. If you are tired, you don't want rich food. As long as he is eating hay he is OK. Feeding soaked hay is a useful way of ensuring that a tired horse rehydrates himself.

9

Lameness, injury and first aid

Detection of Lameness

As with the selection of a horse for purchase, it is important to have a series of questions that you ask yourself as you try to pinpoint the area of pain. This way you can proceed in a logical fashion and not miss out subtle physical evidence. You must systematically evaluate the horse so that the source(s) of pain can be located. In this way the cause of lameness can be identified and a rational treatment can be given.

Points to Consider

- Age
- Breed
- Shoeing
- Occupation
- History
- Fitness
- Movement
- Conformation
- Remember: most foreleg lameness is in the foot

Examination at Rest

Don't be in a hurry to get the horse out of the stable. You can learn a lot by close observation at rest. Remember to record:

- location of visible injuries
- the symmetry of the horse: is one hipbone more prominent; is one hoof bigger than the other?
- stance: is the horse trying to 'save' one limb?
- is there a defect in conformation likely to cause weakness and problems?
- temperament

Your hands can tell you a great deal. Use them to assess:

- hoof balance, pick up the feet and check sole, frog, heels, wall and coronet. How long ago was the horse shod?
- feel for heat, swelling and pain in joints, long bones, tendons and ligaments
- feel for equal contour, consistency and sensitivity of shoulders, hips and stifles

Try not to prejudge the situation. An old injury may be unsightly but cause no problems.

Examination when Moving

Ensure that the horse is suitably restrained before you take it out of the stable. A head collar may not be adequate to hold a hyped-up horse that has been on box-rest for several days! A hard, level surface is ideal so that you can hear the footfalls clearly, and make sure your assistant allows the horse to move its head and neck freely; slight unevenness can be cleverly disguised by holding the horse's head up.

In Walk

- initially watch the whole horse rather than specific areas
- then watch how the feet are placed on the ground
- watch the flight of the leg
- check the relative stride length
- see if one fetlock sinks abnormally
- observe the turns carefully

At Trot

- watch the head carriage for 'nodding'; as the sound foreleg hits the ground, the head will dip down as weight is taken off the lame leg and the horse lands heavily on the sound leg — listen!
- observe freedom of action — it will be 'pottery' if both forelegs are affected
- check for dragging of toes
- check for asymmetrical movement of the quarters as a sound hind leg compensates for a lame leg
- is the trot affected by: hard ground, soft ground, up hill, down hill, sudden starts, sudden stops?

Small Circles at Walk

The horse should be pulled towards the handler in as small a circle as possible.

- watch for hind legs crossing over equally on both reins
- check flexibility

Larger Circles on Lunge

- foreleg lameness is exaggerated when the affected leg is on the inside
- diagnosis of hind leg lameness does not follow any set rules!

Ridden Exercise

- will exaggerate hind leg lameness particularly when rider is sitting on diagonal of affected leg
- bridle lameness may be an evasion

Aggravation of the Lameness

This is probably a job for the vet but can be carried out by the experienced horseman. Lameness may be increased by:

- hoof tester pressure
- finger pressure on bone, e.g. splints
- finger pressure on tendons and ligaments: always do both legs
- flexion tests: flex the joint for 60 seconds then trot the horse away. Remember that it may be difficult to flex only one joint and that the horse may normally take two or three lame steps

Further Tests

If the source of pain or the seat of lameness cannot be identified, further tests can be carried out by the vet. These include:

- nerve blocks
- bone and tendon scans
- faradism to test for muscle pain
- x-rays
- blood tests
- surgery

Remember that, if the horse has been carrying less weight on one limb for some time, he will have developed a high degree of muscle imbalance. This will show when you look at him from the back and the front, and if you compare and feel the muscles you will find that the horse is not evenly developed. Consequently an abnormal gait pattern can develop quite slowly over a period of time and can result in lameness either from strain on the other limb which is doing extra work or from the back, pelvis or shoulders compensating for the lack of strength and power in the unbalanced muscle groups.

Never forget the truth of the old saying, 'ninety per cent of lameness is in the foot.' We know that, if the foot is not taking its share of the weight in the stance phase of the stride, then the horse's body will compensate for this. Although the compensation may be slight, the horse will eventually develop problems in his back, shoulders and pelvis — all due to his feet. Of course this can be the other way round, with back muscle problems causing gait abnormalities.

The more care and attention you give and the more regular monitoring and profile recording you do, the greater will be the benefit to your horse as they will provide an early warning system. Prevention is always better than cure!

Injury

Wound Healing and the Inflammatory Process

Whatever the injury the healing process is the same. An understanding of the way the process occurs will enable the horse owner to treat the injury correctly and also to determine whether veterinary attention is necessary.

Healing has three distinct phases: regeneration or organisation, repair and remodelling. The regeneration and repair can occur in two different ways. The preferred way is healing by 'first intention'. The edges of the wound are held together and quickly stick to each other. Healing by 'second intention' is a much longer process and occurs when the edges of the wound cannot be held together due to loss of tissue, infection or movement of the wound. Healing then has to wait until the wound is filled with new tissue; only then can new skin grow over the surface.

In all but very minor injuries, bleeding or haemorrhage is the first step in the healing process. Blood leaks from the broken blood vessels into the damaged area and quickly clots in an attempt to seal the injury. The clot is made up of fibrin and red and white blood cells.

A wound is like a burning building. The alarm is sounded, the fire brigade arrives and puts out the fire; the demolition experts remove the debris; and the builders repair and restore the building. These steps begin with the inflammatory process. Inflammation is essential: wound repair and healing must be preceded by inflammation. However, if the process becomes excessive, then inflammation can be harmful and delay healing. It is important when treating wounds and injuries that the inflammatory process be controlled.

Inflammation is the body's way of trying to destroy, dilute and wall off from the rest of the body any irritating agent; it is actually partly a defence process. The signs of inflammation are *redness*, *swelling*, *heat* and *pain*. The redness is due to an increased blood flow to the area and occurs almost instantly: scratch the back of your hand and red weals appear almost straight away. The area swells because fluid seeps from the blood vessels and floods the site surrounding the wound. This swelling or oedema can be very extensive in bruised and lacerated wounds. The wound will be hot, partly as a result of the increased blood flow and partly because of the metabolic reactions taking place which create heat. Nature ensures that wounds are painful so that the animal is discouraged from using the damaged area. This means that it may not be beneficial to eliminate pain totally. The pain is caused by increased pressure on pain receptors due to the swelling. This is particularly obvious in a foot injury where swelling is contained within the rigid hoof causing severe lameness. The inflammatory response also causes the release of poisons such as *prostaglandins* which cause nerve irritation and pain.

The first stage of the inflammatory reaction is dependent on a substance called *histamine*. Damaged cells release histamine which causes the tiny blood capillaries to expand or dilate in the area local to the wound. As the walls of the capillaries stretch, various components of the blood are allowed to escape in order of size. These cells and fluid cause swelling. The escapees include globulins, antibodies, polymorphs and fibrinogen. The *globulins* are blood proteins and bring with them *antibodies* to fight *antigens* or foreign proteins which may be present in the wound. The *polymorphs* are special white blood cells that have a *phagocytic* role. In other words they ingest and carry away foreign bodies or bacteria or they can produce substances that liquefy damaged tissue so that it can be absorbed. The polymorphs are the fire brigade attempting to put out the fire. *Fibrinogen* is also released from the blood and starts to wall off the damaged area from the rest of the body by forming a clot.

The leaking of plasma into the injured area has several other effects. The fluid dilutes the toxic effect of any infecting bacteria making their effect less damaging; the high concentration of salts in the plasma causes water to be drawn to the area, contributing to the swelling; and the presence of plasma contents stimulates the lymphatic system to promote drainage away from the area. However, excessive leakage can actually reduce blood pressure and contribute to any shock symptoms that the horse may be showing. In these severe cases inflammation can be partly controlled by antihistamine treatment.

About 30 minutes after the injury has occurred, the inflammatory process enters the second or histamine-independent stage. The state of capillary dilation is maintained by vasoactive proteins which counter the effect of the body's natural inflammation inhibitors, e.g. adrenaline. Normally an animal subject to injury also feels fear, which leads to the release of the 'flight or fight' hormone adrenaline. One of the effects of adrenaline is to cause vasoconstriction so that blood can be diverted to the skeletal muscles activating them for flight. However, in this case vasoconstriction would be counterproductive to the healing process so vasodilation is maintained. In serious injuries it is often necessary for the vet or owner to intervene and control the amount of inflammation because the swelling can lead to permanent distension especially in the horse's lower limb where circulation is poor. It has been said that nature contributes 95% to healing, but the 5% that the vet contributes is vital, particularly towards controlling the inflammatory process.

As phagocytosis continues, the damaged area begins to shrink and new blood vessels and tissue cells start to invade the area and replace the clot. This process of regeneration or repair will vary depending on the tissue involved; for example, epithelial tissue, such as the epidermis of the skin or the lining of the gut, regenerates very easily so that the new tissue appears identical to the old tissue before it was damaged. In fact all epithelium is being replaced continuously. Thus a superficial abrasion that leaves the blood vessels intact heals without scarring, but deeper wounds that interfere with the blood supply often result in scar formation in the connective tissue and leave the epidermis thinner and more susceptible to future injury. Thus, for example, a wound under the saddle may be more sensitive after healing.

Epidermal cells from the skin follow the polymorph invasion and form a thin layer of new skin under the scab covering the wound. In clean-cut wounds, where the edges of the wound are very close together, this process takes 24 to 40 hours but it obviously takes much longer in larger, deeper wounds. The thin layer takes about a week to develop and differentiate into a layer of fragile skin.

A similar process is occurring in the depths of the wound where cells called *fibroblasts* migrate to the area and start to multiply. These cells are involved in the manufacture of *connective tissue*, which is the tissue that connects skin to underlying organs and gives muscle, tendons and ligaments their strength. Division of the fibroblasts gives rise to rope-like strands of *fibrin* at a rate of about one-tenth of an inch a day. Further fibroblasts can then migrate into the wound along the fibrin which acts like a scaffold for healing tissue to build upon. The fibroblasts also lay down strands of tough collagen scar tissue which meet in the middle of a typical surgical wound in about a week.

The next phase of repair is to establish a new blood circulation in the damaged area. *Endothelial cells* originating from the damaged capil-

laries at the edge of the wound push their way into the damaged site
and multiply to form branching buds of tissue which burrow into the
damaged site following the fibrin strands. A primitive blood circulation
becomes established and in a few days the original blood clot becomes
a highly vascular, quickly growing mass called *granulation tissue*.

A system of lymphatic vessels grows in parallel to the blood vessels
to 'mop up' any leakage from the new circulation and return it to the
venous circulation. As the fibroblasts lay down more collagen, the
blood vessels decrease in number, the white blood cells disappear and
then, as the collagen contracts, the wound gets smaller and the repair
stronger. Eventually elastic fibres replace some of the collagen, making the wound more pliable, and feeling returns as nerve fibres grow
into the scar. Once the wound has a blood, lymphatic and nerve supply
and a collagen-building system, it is effectively healed but now has to
undergo a remodelling process so that the damaged tissue is returned
to its normal pre-injury state.

The success of the first part of wound healing, i.e. repair and regeneration, is dependent on good first aid:

- control of bleeding
- cleanliness
- bandaging/suturing
- control of inflammation

The second part of healing, remodelling, has been neglected in the
past and is where controlled exercise and physiotherapy can be
enormously useful.

Repair

Most soft tissues other than epithelial cells tend to have a slow turnover
rate and to be quite complex, containing specialised cells and collagen
fibres for strength.

Muscle Tissue

Muscle tissue unites by the formation of a scar as described, but many
muscles replace the damaged tissue with fibrous tissue not true muscle
tissue, resulting in an inelastic scar. It is therefore important, that
muscle heals with a scar long enough to allow the muscle to extend
during normal movement, which means that the horse must not be
immobilised during healing. Immobility may also lead to adhesions
forming between muscle fibres, causing further muscle damage during
muscle contraction.

Nervous Tissue

If the branch of a nerve cell is damaged there may be some regrowth of that branch, but if the nerve cell body is damaged it cannot be replaced. This means that recovery from nerve damage is slow and very limited, often leading to permanent disability.

Factors Affecting Healing

Position of the Wound

The position of the wound can be critical as good healing is dependent on the blood supply. If the blood supply is plentiful, e.g. in the face, healing will be faster than if the blood supply is poor, as it is in the lower limb, for example. If the wound is in a position where it is being constantly moved or interfered with by the horse, then healing will also be slowed. It may be necessary to sedate, tie up or put a cradle on a horse to prevent it from licking or biting painful wounds.

Shape of the Wound

In circular, torn wounds the amount of contraction that the wound can undergo will affect the rate of healing. If the skin is loose, wound contraction can significantly reduce the amount of healing needed to cover the wound site. However, there is practically no wound contraction below the knee and hock, and healing of these wounds relies on the slow process of *epithelialisation*. Thus even quite small wounds on the lower leg can be serious. If the contraction process is deficient, there is a greater chance of excess granulation tissue being formed.

Granulation tissue (proud flesh)

Granulation tissue is a normal product of the healing process, and consists of blood vessels, polymorphs and other blood cells. Under most circumstances granulation tissue is filled with fibres, which become cross-linked and increasingly solid to become scar tissue. This process should be confined to an area below the surface of the wound so that epithelial tissue simultaneously grows over the wound followed by wound contraction and collagenisation. Because wound contraction is minimal in the wounds of the lower leg, epithelialisation may not be complete before the granulation tissue has filled the wound. Consequently it grows out over the edges of the wound forming a *granuloma* or proud flesh. Epithelial tissue will not grow over granulation tissue; it has to burrow through the granuloma, a very slow process. As the granuloma overgrows the edges of the wound, the sensitive new epithelium dies and the wound actually gets bigger. It is important to try to prevent proud flesh formation by ensuring that epithelialisation takes place. Good first aid is of paramount importance, and bandaging is useful in maintaining the correct conditions for healing.

Foreign Bodies in Wounds

Foreign particles in a wound harbour bacteria, and, even if sterile, act as irritants by stimulating the inflammatory reaction so that the particle becomes encapsulated in fibrous tissue forming an abscess. The infection will not be healed, and the foreign particle may even move through tissue in an attempt to break out at the surface. A deep, black thorn will eventually come to the surface but may cause persistent lameness on the way which is very difficult to diagnose.

First Aid

Good, immediate first aid by the owner followed by veterinary backup if necessary is vital to good healing. The following guidelines apply to torn and cut wounds where the skin is broken and there is bleeding.

(1)   Control the Bleeding

If the horse can be moved, get it to the stable yard as quickly as possible so that the extent of the damage can be ascertained and the vet can be called if necessary. If the horse cannot be moved, get veterinary assistance as soon as possible and take steps to control the bleeding there and then. Small cuts and grazes are no problem: the torn small arteries and veins quickly contract and stop bleeding; this process can be hastened by gently cold hosing the area to aid in blood vessel contraction. Larger wounds and deep cuts involving large blood vessels can bleed for some time. Arterial bleeding can be very spectacular and distressing, with bright red blood spurting from the wound, whereas venous bleeding is indicated by dark red blood trickling from a wound. Both of these types of bleeding can be controlled by applying pressure to the area; on the leg this could be done by means of a pressure bandage, or, if the wound is on the body, by pressing a clean cloth on to the wound. If there is bad arterial bleeding on a limb, a tourniquet can be tied tightly above the wound but must be released every 15 minutes to ensure that the circulation to the rest of the limb is maintained. Once the bleeding has been controlled, the wound can be cleaned.

(2) Clean the Wound

A contaminated wound takes a long time to heal so thorough cleaning at this initial stage is very important. The area can be syringed or swabbed: do not skimp on the cotton wool, use large, clean swabs, and do not return soiled swabs to the water. Use a large quantity of warm dilute disinfectant such as Eusol to remove dead tissue and dirt. Large particles can be carefully removed with tweezers. The wound should then be covered with an antibiotic spray or powdered and covered with a clean dressing, either to heal on its own or to await veterinary attention. A non-adherent dressing such as Melolin is very useful to place next to the wound as it does not stick and thus impede healing. If the vet has been called, do not apply any proprietary healing ointment or oil because such materials are very difficult to remove should the wound need stitching.

(3) Suturing (Stitching)

The closer the edges of a wound can be kept together, the quicker it will heal. The edges of small wounds can be brought together by bandaging or sticking plaster, but larger wounds — especially deep ones — need stitching. However, stitching is rarely used for ragged wounds where there has been a lot of tissue destruction because these wounds are usually heavily infected and if the exit to the wound is blocked by stitching it may become very septic and healing is delayed. In order to bring the edges of this type of wound together, a great deal of tension must be applied to the stitches and thus the blood supply is limited and healing delayed. Often these stitches are actually pulled apart causing more damage.

The horse may require a general anaesthetic before stitching but a sedative and local anaesthetic may be adequate. The vet will then stop any bleeding that is still occurring by clamping off the bleeding vessels. The wound is cleaned and any dead or damaged tissue is removed or debrided. If necessary, the underlying layers of tissue are stitched into place and finally the same is done to the skin. Suturing is much more successful if the wound lies parallel to the line of strain. Thus, for example, vertical wounds on the leg heal better than those running horizontally. Wounds above the knee and hock heal better than those below due to the poor blood supply, the lack of underlying tissue and the degree of movement. A stitched wound should always remain free draining.

(4) Bandaging

A stitched area on a limb will have to be bandaged for protection. The wound should be dressed with antibiotic powder and a non-adhesive dressing must be placed over the top and held in place with a firmly applied bandage over the top of plenty of padding (gamgee or fibregee). Remember to bandage the opposite leg as well since the horse is likely to favour the injured leg thus putting more strain on the sound leg.

Some wounds, particularly those below the knee and hock, are better bandaged than stitched. In this case a fairly tight pressure bandage is applied over the dressed wound, possibly with a stable bandage over the top. The points in favour of bandaging are:

- it helps keep the wound relatively clean
- it helps keep the wound moist which helps epithelialisation
- it helps protect the wound from further damage, e.g. knocks and bangs
- it limits the amount of bleeding
- it limits the development of proud flesh

Bandaging does have several disadvantages:

- the dressing will to some extent act as an irritant to the exposed sensitive tissue
- bandaging limits the oxygen supply necessary for healing
- a bandage may impede circulation if badly applied
- it can become saturated with pus and provide an excellent breeding ground for bacteria and infection

The preparation of a wound for bandaging is very similar to that already described:

- stop the bleeding
- clean the wound
- apply antibiotic powder or spray and cover with a non-adhesive dressing and a pad of cotton wool
- apply a pressure bandage
- replace every day

It is very tempting to change the dressing more frequently than once a day, but constantly disturbing the wound can actually delay healing. Provided that the wound is cleaned thoroughly and suitable antibiotic therapy is given, the wound should not become infected.

When to Call the Vet

It is sometimes difficult to decide whether to call the vet or to let the horse heal itself. Here are some guidelines indicating when the vet should be called:

(1)   The wound is more than $2\frac{1}{2}$ cm long and penetrates the whole thickness of the skin, and the edges of the wound gape wide.
(2)   The bleeding is so severe that it cannot be controlled by a pressure bandage, particularly if this bleeding is arterial.
(3)   The wound is deep and penetrating.
(4)   The horse has not had a recent tetanus vaccination.

Categories of Wounds

Wounds fall into six main categories and the implications and treatment of each type are different:

- torn or lacerated
- clean cut or incised
- puncture
- bruised or contused
- strain or sprain
- break or fracture

Torn or Lacerated Wounds

This type of wound is frequently encountered and is characterised by the edges of the wound being torn and ragged with a lot of tissue destruction. It is typically caused by a horse getting caught in barbed wire fencing. There is usually little arterial bleeding associated with these tears because, when blood vessels are damaged by tearing, the elastic walls spring back to seal themselves. Tear wounds on the lower leg are difficult to stitch if a lot of tissue has been lost and may be best treated by bandaging. Tear wounds on the abdomen, if stitched, must be allowed to drain freely; protect the horse's skin from the blistering effect of the exudate with petroleum jelly or a similar waterproof preparation. If promptly and correctly treated, these wounds should heal satisfactorily.

Clean-cut or Incised Wounds

As the name suggests, this wound is usually caused by a sharp instrument, for example glass or indeed a vet's scalpel. As there is little tissue damage, this type of wound is easily stitched and usually heals by first intention providing no underlying structures have been damaged. Deep cuts are often associated with a lot of bleeding and may require a tourniquet or *ligature* to stop the flow.

Puncture Wounds

Puncture wounds are caused by long sharp objects, e.g. a nail penetrating the horse. They can be difficult first to locate and secondly to treat because the entry point may be very small and heal rapidly even though underlying tissue and structures have been quite seriously damaged. Typical examples are a horse treading on a nail or its skin being pierced by a sharp twig. In such instances very little evidence of injury may be found superficially but the horse may become very lame or develop a nasty abscess. Puncture wounds also provide an ideal environment for the bacterium causing tetanus.

Bruised or Contused Wounds

Bruises are often found in conjunction with lacerated wounds and are caused by falls, kicks and collisions. As the horse is covered in hair and has a thick skin, it is difficult to actually see bruises as one can in humans. Remember that they are still there and may caused lameness and discomfort in horses for several days after an accident or injury.

Strains and Sprains

The term 'strain' tends to be associated with tendon injury whereas 'sprain' refers to joints and ligaments. Both terms refer to damage and tearing of the collagen fibres within the tendon or ligament causing inflammation characterised by variable degrees of heat, swelling and lameness.

Breaks or Fractures

Bones appear to be good at repairing breaks and remodelling the subsequent callus so that very little evidence of damage remains. However, correct healing can only occur if the broken bone is immobilised, which poses a major problem in horses and can lead to many other problems such as muscle wastage.

10
Sports therapy and fitness

Fitness and Performance

We can define fitness as being a state in which the body and mind can maintain a balance of health in order that the work which the body is called upon to perform can be carried out without causing undue stress. The requirement may be just a simple walk for a short period, or, at the other end of the scale, we may have an athlete performing at the highest level of speed or endurance. Both need only to be fit enough to carry out their respective activities efficiently: they can perform to their satisfaction and yet still maintain their existing health and fitness levels.

It is important to appreciate that all exertion including fitness training can cause microscopic tearing of tissue cells. The result of this stress will trigger the brain to inform the cells of the need to respond and develop. This is how increased strength and resilience are achieved. Stress is essential to survival; it results in the horse's body and mind adapting so that next time that particular stress arises it is dealt with efficiently and it is no longer stressful. What must be avoided is over-stress. Overstress occurs when the cells are too damaged to respond to the demands, or when the communications between the brain and the nerve cells are not being clearly received.

Fitness levels are often assessed purely from a cardiovascular point of view, in other words by the response to exercise in terms of heart rate and recovery rates. These criteria are good indicators of general fitness. However, we should look at fitness in its totality including all the systems involved with movement: nervous, muscular, connective and skeletal systems and their co-ordination. The soft tissues of the body are the source of a great deal of discomfort, and it is not always appreciated that they are a real limiting factor in performance potential. A stiff and aching body or part does not encourage athleticism.

There is no point having a perfectly tuned engine (heart and lungs) without adequate transmission to the wheels (muscles). The heart may be able to pump the blood to the muscles, but if a muscle is unable to contract fully, or cannot release fully from a contracted state, the horse will not move properly. Hence repair and healing will not take place efficiently as blood will not be able to enter the tense muscle area, and thus the horse will not be fit enough to do his job.

If a muscle in a group of muscles is not working in balance, the joint or tendon which the muscles support and protect is at risk; the horse is only as strong as his weakest point. Remember that the role of the muscles, as well as causing movement, is to control and to prevent movement.

Proper training and performing will result in some pain and discomfort. As Jane Fonda would say, 'No pain, no gain'. To increase fitness it is necessary to push the body a little bit more at each training session, giving stimuli that encourage the body to develop in such a way that it can cope with this increased stress. It is a gradual process. There is a very fine balance that must be maintained: you must push to get response, but, if you overdo it, healing and repair will not remain in balance. Full repair will not have taken place before the next training session. So, each time the body is asked to perform, the still slightly damaged tissue will suffer a little more and there will be a corresponding increase in the pain and discomfort until such a time as it cannot respond to the demands freely and we have an unlevel or lame horse to deal with. The animal will not be happy and well disposed to work. Hence interval training or fast work only takes place twice a week allowing time for recovery between each session.

Performance and Injury

So many good equine performers are lost because their attitude to work has deteriorated due to pain and discomfort from training and performing. The horse goes off form, and it is no longer able to give, or wishes to give, the effort needed to perform. It becomes increasingly insecure, loses confidence in itself and its rider, and becomes more prone to accidents.

There is now much more understanding of total fitness which can be used to aid the athlete to improve his performance so that he can compete longer and more consistently. This is especially so for human beings. The sprinter does not merely sprint in training; he uses weights to improve his torso and arms so that his entire body is fit and trained. The same advantages can be given to the equine athlete, and the increased benefits enable us to bring out his full potential.

Let us look at what has happened following a hard performance. The horse will have minor muscle damage from exertion: the waste created, for example lactic acid, may not yet have been fully cleared because the circulation has been clogged up by the influx of lymph and enzymes as a response to inflammation. These minor injuries to the tissue have started a minor inflammatory response. The increased circulation brings fibroblasts to help the healing process. These can also stick the muscle fibres and the connective tissue together, clogging the system even more. The muscles are tight and sore, and the horse feels stiff and will move less, further reducing the circulation. The clogging and swelling may also cause pressure on the nerve endings, giving rise to more discomfort, and the horse will take up a protective posture which compounds the problems. The well developed outline needed to perform well is not maintained as the horse tries to compensate for his discomfort. Little by little this leads to the state when the horse goes off form. He may even be abused because he is becoming evasive to the demands of the rider. His normally good, cooperative temperament no longer aims to please: instinct has taken over, and self-preservation becomes the sole motivation and the main influence on his work.

The Role of Sports Therapy

Thus there is the need to provide the equine athlete with relevant therapy which the human athlete already enjoys; but of course taking account of the fundamental differences between horse and man.

Sports therapy can support and maintain overall fitness, prevent injury, speed up and make the important recovery period more effective, and ensure that the soft tissue is working fully. It also ensures that the vital circulation is functioning correctly so that the natural repair and healing processes are given all the help they need. The horse therefore does not experience stiffness and pain for too long, and he recovers quickly and completely before his next exertion. This sort of expertise may seem expensive, but it can save money and is good common sense. Ask a human athlete if he would perform without it. The human being can carry out some of his own sports therapy himself but the horse cannot. However, his owner/rider can do a great deal and the effort can be rewarding. Without some professional therapy training, however, and an in-depth knowledge of the horse and its structure and of his development and training, as well as experience in caring for equine athletes, the owner/rider cannot be expected to achieve the same results as a qualified equine sports therapist.

This is why equine sports therapy is being developed: to ensure that the trained person has all the necessary knowledge of the horse, of his training and management, and of the application of the various therapies and techniques. Equine sports therapy covers many aspects, and regular treatment of healthy equine athletes before competition, during training and after exertion will certainly be of great benefit. Keeping the horse cardiovascularly fit during periods of inactivity, for example while recovering from injury or when he is unable to carry out a normal training programme, is also an important part of sports therapy.

Remedial Work

Another aspect is remedial work, including developing or redeveloping correct posture and action. Remedial work should result in the more economical use of the horse's energy in his athletic pursuits. Any horse that has been unlevel or lame for a period, even for as short a time as a week, will have muscle imbalance and will perhaps make some form of compensation. This will very rarely correct itself and will produce strain and limit performance. The equine sports therapist's role includes preventing these imbalances occurring and giving remedial treatment if they have arisen.

First Aid

A knowledge of first aid is also a very important part of sports therapy and, as with with humans, is considered to be one of the main factors in the ultimate speed and quality of the repair. It must, however, be applied as soon as possible after injury. The treatment is only *first aid* and is not a substitute for veterinary treatment.

Although the equine sports therapist's main aim is to bring out the full athletic potential of the horse, he or she will also work closely with your veterinary surgeon, carrying out his recommended treatment for injuries. Many horses have successfully healed after a bad injury but never quite display their former brilliance. This may be due to subtle changes in muscle balance and poor internal healing with adhesions limiting movement.

The injured athlete is looking for complete recovery with no limiting factors in the healing. Full recovery from any injury will need an individual rehabilitation programme.

Types of Sports Therapy

There are many forms of sports therapy and it is useful to identify which ones the rider/owner/trainer can carry out himself and which are better left to an appropriately qualified person. Usually it is a shared operation.

Apart from the obvious use of the hands, the following form part of the functions of the sports therapist:

Application of heat	Hydrotherapies
Special exercises	Cold therapies
Bandaging and support	Movement analyses
Nutrition	Food additives
Herbal nutrition	Homeopathy
Ground schooling	Development tack
Treadmill work	Fitness monitoring
Heart-rate monitoring	General environmental care
Performance care	First aid
Horse psychology	Foot-balancing analysis

All these can be used to aid in the general development and care of the horse. The veterinary surgeon may also recommend the use of these therapies on injured horses. His approval must be sought before using electrotherapy, including the use of lasers, ultrasound, acupuncture or chiropractic manipulation.

In all cases it is best to talk to your vet and your trainer and discuss what you wish to do. The aim is to produce a horse which can give you pleasure in his performance at whatever level, and this means team effort, the team comprising horse, rider, trainer, groom, farrier, vet and sports therapist. Many of these professional people are, or have been, athletes themselves, and may have experienced problems from injuries. Some may have benefited from sports therapy and appreciate the extra attention that has brought about their complete recovery.

In this chapter we will look at several types of sports therapy, enabling you to understand more about the principles involved; what they can and cannot do; and which ones are dangerous in use. You may not be able to achieve satisfactory results yourself, but you will know what is available and what results can be expected. In some cases these practices are very easy to carry out. The real expertise is knowing when and how they are to be used. A knowledge of the horse's anatomy and biomechanics is essential.

Soft Tissue Manipulation and Massage

Soft tissue manipulation and sports massage are but two well established methods used by sportsmen and women, and the benefits are well known. With the advent of new technology and the increase in the use of machines, these techniques are seen by some as old fashioned and unsophisticated, not to mention hard work! Nevertheless, they are techniques which have stood the test of time and are very effective if learned well and practised properly. However skilled one may be in these techniques, the results will depend upon the therapist's skill in palpation. Anybody can learn to massage, but the skill lies in knowing how much pressure to apply and for how long, remembering our equine friend cannot talk to us. Thus 'feel' is very important.

Here we see the fundamental difference between the equine and the human therapist. The equine therapist must initially communicate with the horse through his or her hands. Human beings are able to say if something is not quite right, or not as good as it should be. The equine therapist must explore the soft tissues very intimately with trained hands. He or she will detect the effects of strenuous activity, monitor the different stresses in the tissues, and find variations and interpret what they mean, even if there is no sign of a problem either in action or in movement.

The equine therapist must spend a great deal of time learning how to palpate, educating the hands to know exactly what tissues lie underneath. He or she must be able to identify the quality and state of the tissue and know what attention is required, if any.

Timing of palpation is important. There is great benefit to be obtained in doing this before and after strenuous activity to make sure everything is functioning properly, as well as routinely during the training programme. The more one handles any animal the more one becomes aware of its individual tissue response to exertion and fatigue. Any necessary action can then be taken early to prevent minor matters from becoming major problems. Here the therapist is not looking for major problems but trying to ensure that the athletic function is normal and that no limitations have occurred. Prevention of injury is a major role of the sports therapist.

The expert can tell you the state of the horse's soft tissue: whether there is any tension, lack of tone, tightness and loss of freedom from small adhesions. The therapist should also assess the state of the nerve reflexes, whether there is any congestion restricting the circulation, and whether there is scarring, fibrosis, stress, spasms, inelasticity, inflammation, etc. Any change in balance and any weight redistribution will also be noted.

You will appreciate that competition and training will push a horse to the limits of fatigue. As standards of competition increase, we must do all we can to keep him fit enough to enjoy the work he is doing, to show improvement and to give consistent performance. This will increase his confidence and skill, and make him as safe as possible and accident free.

The horse must recover fully from the effects of fatigue as quickly as possible otherwise these will accumulate, reducing his standard of performance, and overuse injuries will result. The rest times between periods of activity are therefore very important, and must be made as effective as possible. It is the quality of the rest period that is the most important factor ensuring complete recovery after exertion, not necessarily the length of the period.

There are some problems which are obvious and which are dealt with straight away by first aid or by referral to the veterinary surgeon. The accumulative problems mentioned above may not be evident until the horse is actually under performance stress. He may not be lame or moving badly but he cannot give the extra exertion needed to perform well, and this only becomes apparent during testing performance. This is where he becomes vulnerable to accidents and injury. Signs of incomplete recovery are very subtle and may not manifest clinically, but can disturb the vital rest period.

If recovery after the rest period is manifestly incomplete, it usually means that complete recovery has not been taking place for some time. Symptoms would include restlessness, constant changing of position, different stance and behaviour in the stable, changes in jumping or movement techniques, and changes in facial expression, habits or temperament. The quality of the rest period is paramount, and the ministrations of the therapist are very important in ensuring that this is so. The hands are used in soft tissue manipulation, which is an essential service in the prevention of athletic injuries.

Manipulation can influence the tissues in different ways depending on the time that has elapsed since performance and on the extent of the damage. Massage, with the action of the hands over the skin, will cause friction which will produce some heat in the underlying tissues as they are moved upon each other. This will dilate the arterioles and the capillaries, and with the stimulation of the axonal reflexes will improve the circulation from the deeper tissue to the superficial parts.

All these effects will help to restore elasticity to the tissue and assist in the nutrition of the cells and the removal of the increased waste products caused by exertion. Heat can be obtained by the use of massage or by other means. It is, however, beneficial to use the hands in massage for two reasons. First, it can form part of your palpation investigations on the state of the tissue and, secondly, it can, if done gently, induce relaxation to a fatigued body and quieten the mind which has been excited and cannot settle down. General fatigue can affect the brain, which will keep the body tense and overstress the immune system. This psychological relaxation is therefore an important matter. Anxiety produces physical reactions in the soft tissues, and if these are sustained a chain reaction will be set up which can be difficult to control, further depleting the immune system. Think how susceptible we are to minor colds and ailments if we are tired and overstressed.

Manipulation can produce other benefits which in their nature are mechanical, physiological and reflex. Stimulation to the exteroceptors and the proprioceptors is provided. Exteroceptors are nerve endings in the skin stimulated by the immediate external environment, and proprioceptors give information about movement and position of the body and are mainly in the muscles and tendons.

The hands can assist the tissue by their pressure on the venous and lymphatic systems, thus increasing the circulation. By causing increased pressure in the vessels in front of the hand, a vacuum is formed in those behind, thus making room for fluid coming from the deeper tissues. This results in an increase in the venous pressure, creating a situation in which increased circulation takes place with a corresponding increase in the total arterial blood supply to the parts being treated.

The red cell count increases after soft tissue manipulation. This means that there will be more haemoglobin for oxygen transportation. Increasing the aerobic capacity of the horse, that is, his ability to transport and utilise oxygen in the body, is a major aim of a training programme. Oxygen is an essential tissue nutrient and vital to tissue healing. Increasing the efficiency of blood and lymph circulation will help in the prevention of oedema which, if not dispersed, will cause pressure and the tissue will become stretched.

The therapist's hands can stretch the muscle fibres in all directions, not only in the normal direction of the muscle action. They will also move the muscle bundles away from each other, preventing small adhesions from forming which will glue the bundles together and restrict their functions. Again this will improve the circulation within the muscles and prevent muscle tissue from becoming tight and inelastic. Tight muscles have a reduced circulation, and are consequently deprived of nutrition. There will also be an accumulation of waste products such as lactic acid, causing discomfort and pain. If unchecked, the horse's attitude to work will suffer.

Any disruption of the electrical activity that balance all biological activities within the tissue will also be reduced by massage. If this delicate electrical balance is upset, healing will be delayed and the horse's recovery will take longer. Once the tissue has been manipulated and is feeling free from tension, and a good circulation has been re-established, the therapist can move the horse's limbs through their normal range of movement to stretch the muscles. First of all, the front limb is lifted and all joints are moved gently to their comfortable limit. The limb is then taken backwards and, again, eased only to its comfortable limit. It is then taken forwards, eased and encouraged to stretch as much as it can (Fig. 10.1).

The same procedure is carried out on the hind limbs: the joints are flexed, the limb is taken forwards and out behind. The stretching of the hind limbs will also have a beneficial effect on the horse's back as it

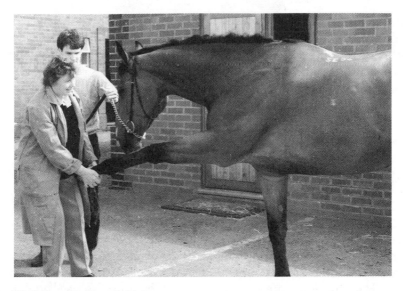

Fig. 10.1 Fore limb stretching.

also will be stretched. Horses will enjoy this and can learn to assist in the exercises.

It will be of advantage to the horse to take the limbs through their full range of movements before work. Note any limitations and, if these do not improve, make sure that he is subsequently given proper rehabilitation and that his work is adjusted.

All these ministrations should be timed very carefully. When treating a horse after extreme activity, it may be advantageous to see him immediately following his initial recovery when he has stopped blowing and has cooled down. Some individuals may benefit from being looked at several hours afterwards, depending on the effects of the exertion.

The importance of cooling down after exertion is not always fully appreciated. The horse needs to be kept moving and allowed to stretch to allow his circulation to slow down gradually. If the circulation slows too quickly, the waste products of exercise may become trapped within the muscle. He should be protected from extremes of heat and cold. Recovery has not finished until the horse's respiration, heart rate and temperature have returned to normal and he has stopped sweating. He can then be taken back to his box to be washed and made comfortable. Under hot, humid conditions cooling the horse properly is of paramount importance. If, for any reason, the horse has not been able to cool down in the normal way, he is more likely to be stiff and sore. Under these circumstances he can be made more comfortable by the sports therapist. If he has been injured, he must receive the necessary veterinary treatment and then the rest of his body can be given proper support by the sports therapist to lessen the overall stress. This general support will in itself help the injury to heal more quickly.

Some owners like to use therapeutic machines to aid the recovery of their horses. Unfortunately, many people who own machines do not fully understand the benefits or when and how they should be used. These machines will be looked at in more detail later.

Methods of Soft Tissue Manipulation

Standard techniques with the hands are used such as effleurage, petrissage, friction, deep friction, cross-fibre friction, neurofriction, pressure, tapotement, shaking, vibration, muscle energy techniques (MET), stretching, acupressure, trigger point therapy and zone therapy. Each different technique has its purpose. It is the therapist's responsibility to judge, from the tissue underneath, which techniques to use, how deep to apply the pressure, how much to stretch and when to change the techniques. Lubricants should be used where there is any chance of friction that will make the skin sore.

Remedial massage is hard work, and part of the therapist's training is to use his or her own body to the best advantage, to adjust the touch, the pressure and movement to the tissue under the hands, and to know what is normal reaction in the tissue. If at any time something is felt under one's hands which is beyond one's experience, or appears to be abnormal, it should be referred to the vet before continuing, even if he has asked you to carry out the treatment. Technique, not muscle strength, is required. The amount of time spent is dependent upon the state of the tissues and what one is hoping to achieve at the time.

Effleurage

This is a stroking movement carried out in a rhythmical way and is usually used to start a session because it is the stroke from which your hand will receive information. Effleurage can be done with the whole of the hand, or with the thumb, fingers, the ulnar part of the fist and palm, the heel of the hand, the knuckles, the elbow, and the forearm. Pressure can be superficial or deep or a mixture of both.

Petrissage

This is the ringing, squeezing, rolling, kneading, lifting and stretching of the muscle bellies and their compartments and the connective tissue. It is not meant to pinch or bruise. It can be done with the hands or the fingers, and the degree of movement and pressure depend upon the animal and the state of the tissues.

The action can serve to 'milk' the muscles of the waste products of activity, prevent the formation of tightness and adhesions, and prevent joint restrictions. The stretching is done in all directions, not just in the way that stretching would occur from normal body movement.

Friction

Friction is used for the deeper tissues to 'clean out' joint spaces and around muscle and tendon insertions. It is very effective in making old scar tissue more supple and in breaking down adhesions under the skin and connective tissue and between the muscle compartments. Deep pressure can be applied, and in some areas benefit can be obtained by keeping the pressure applied for some time. Sometimes these tender points are *'trigger'* points and the focus of referred pain. On applying pressure to these points, one can cause a reflex action that encourages muscle relaxation.

Tapotement

This is using the hands and the fingers in a flicking, hacking and pounding action. It is usually carried out before activity, to stimulate the tissue. If can be beneficial when used during a series of activities, to avoid relaxation and cooling down too quickly.

The Application of Heat (Thermotherapy)

Heating of the tissues can be achieved by use of the hands, but it can also be brought about by conductive heat, in other words by the application of hot pads, bottles, heated blankets, hot poultices and hot fomentations. Radiant heat can be provided by infrared light or radiant heat lamps. Heat can also be produced by the use of machines. The choice really depends on the availability and convenience of application and the depth of penetration required.

The effects of heat

The application of heat raises the temperature of the tissue which increases metabolic rate stimulating the repair process. Blood flow is improved with a corresponding increase in the excretion of waste products. Heat can also induce relaxation and increases the efficiency of muscle action; together with the increased blood supply, this ensures that the muscles are in a good condition for contraction. Pressure from congestion in the tissue can cause pain from the pressure on nerves:

heat can help to disperse this congestion relieving the pain. Mild heat has a soothing effect on the sensory nerves, but too high a temperature will cause irritation.

When an area of the skin is exposed to heat, there is an increased stimulation of sweat glands and sensory nerve endings in that area and the heated blood that is circulating around the body influences the centres that control and regulate body temperature. This will increase the activity of the sweat glands which will also help to eliminate waste products through the skin.

Prolonged heat can cause congestion, turning the beneficial effects to harmful ones, and of course burning can take place. Heat causes dilation of the blood vessels situated in the heated area. However, after about 15–20 minutes a reflex vasoconstriction occurs so that blood flow is reduced and congestion can occur. Heat should not be applied for more than half an hour at a time as changes in the metabolic rate in the tissue will take place, especially if the temperature is high. Heat should not be used as a first aid treatment, and a good rule is only to use it when inflammation has finished. In other words do not apply hot treatments until the heat caused by the inflammatory process has gone.

Do not use heat on open wounds. Wash the wound in warm water to clean it and then, once the wound has closed, heat can be used to help the other tissues that were damaged at the same time. The use of lasers can aid wound healing; this will be discussed later.

Heat lamps

Horses which are fatigued often have difficulty in keeping their body temperature at a comfortable level and break out in cold sweats. Such an animal can be helped by the use of heat lamps. The box should be warm so that he can be without clothing except perhaps an open sweat rug. A horse which is fatigued is not helped if he is weighed down by heavy blankets and rugs.

The day following exertion the horse may benefit from a number of sessions under the infrared lamps. After the horse has been under the infrared lamps, allow him to lose heat slowly before he is taken outside, especially if the weather is cold or windy. Then give him a short brisk walk or jog to check his soundness and to help the healing process take place as quickly as possible. If he can be turned out for some period, this will also help to stretch his muscles.

Horses that get very stiff the day after *any* work will benefit from ten minutes under the heat lamps just *before* work commences. Longer periods are not recommended as the horse can become too relaxed instead of just being warmed up for action!

Using heat lamps during operations such as clipping or cold hosing a leg is a good idea. Too often horses with stressed limbs, which are also giving some stress to the body which is trying to heal them, stand in cold boxes or breezy yards with ice or cold water on their legs. Horses that are tired from a previous days' activity are very vulnerable to small stresses and need all their energy for complete recovery.

Heat lamps should be positioned about 18 in (46 cm) away from the part to be treated. As some tissues are more sensitive to heat than others, horses should not be left unattended and a close eye should be kept on the treatment area to avoid over-exposure. The lamps should be protected by a grid so that a bulb cannot be knocked and broken and so that if the bulb shatters it is less likely to cause damage.

Heat lamps are sometimes used to dry horses after washing or swimming. This is not recommended because if the horse is wet there is a greater risk of the tissues becoming too hot. After swimming, which is a very active exercise, the horse is better scraped off and a special rug which absorbs damp put on. The horse should then be walked or exercised to allow the circulation to slow down naturally. Exercise is by far the better method. If the animal is lame and cannot move well, he must be put under the heat lamps or into a drying box. Towel-dry him as much as possible, giving him a good rubbing starting at the lower limbs, bandage as soon as possible to keep his legs warm, and then put on sufficient absorbent rugs depending on the weather.

Ultraviolet lamps are a poor second best to natural sunlight but there are times when horses cannot get outside and therefore get very little sunlight. Some horses are kept in indoor yards and are exercised indoors and do not go outside at all. In these situations there may be a good reason to include ultraviolet light to help the horse's body manufacture vitamin D. If ultraviolet lamps are to be employed, they must be introduced gradually so that the horse becomes used to them over a period of time.

There is a lovely story about a breeder and trainer in Ireland. He was very learned in the influences of the planets and had all his horses' horoscopes prepared at their birth. These horses were only allowed to breed or race on days shown on their charts to be auspicious. He also believed that a horse is influenced by the sun and the sky as well as the stars and planets, so he opened the roofs of their boxes not only on fine days to receive full advantage from the sun but also on nights to receive the advantages that the positioning of the stars and planets could offer! He was a very successful breeder and trainer!

Hydrotherapy

Hydrotherapy includes any treatment using water as an agent, a physical support, a specific therapy or a general rehabilitation exercise, for example swimming, water walks, a jacuzzi and water treadmills.

The physical properties of water, including *buoyancy*, *hydrostatic* pressure and *cohesion*, make it a valuable medium for exercise, and it can play an important part in maintaining and supporting performance and fitness.

A horse needing to maintain muscle, wind and circulatory fitness, but which is temporarily lame, or one that cannot endure the mechanical stress of a traditional training programme, is a typical candidate for the benefits of swimming. A horse which is suffering from the effects of 'wear and tear' or has mechanical conformation defects, but which has real talent and 'heart', can be greatly assisted by swimming. Overweight horses which would put too much stress on their legs if given normal exercise will also benefit. Swimming works very well for reducing the effects of 'competition staleness' or for overtrained horses which take a long time to recover from exertion.

Horses with psychological difficulties have been transformed through swimming as a part of a routine fitness programme. These difficulties may have been at a physical level, causing psychological reactions. Swimming has helped quite a few of these 'problem horses' to compete and perform well.

The physical properties of water can be summarised as follows:

- *Buoyancy* almost eliminates the force of gravity, and the supporting effects may be increased further by artificial appliances.
- *Hydrostatic pressure* is an upward pressure exerted on a body in the water. It is increased in direct proportion to the depth and the density of the water. Hydrostatic pressure is approximately 0.85 lb per sq in for every foot depth of water.
- *The cohesive property* of water, because of the strong attraction of fluid molecules to each other, will give equal resistance in all directions. This will only be altered in relation to the speed of movement of the body going through the water.

Swimming

The remedial advantages of swimming

The absence of weight on the limbs means that movement under water is less painful and joints can move more freely using their full range of movement. If a joint does not move, it will soon deteriorate even if it was not the original cause of the lack of movement.

Elimination of friction on joints encourages the full range of movement. Swimming is a particularly useful way of encouraging the horse to use his joints as part of a rehabilitation programme after injury.

The constant pressure from the water exerted on the limbs will also assist the venous and lymphatic return flow, and this increases correspondingly with any workload increase. Some researchers believe that many problems with horses' limbs and feet are aggravated by insufficient circulation, especially when related to the amount of work expected from the horse. This is not helped if the horse is standing in its stable for hours at a time and his exercise periods are short and intense. Swimming will give rise to good circulation to these areas without concussion from ground contact.

If muscles are kept in use, problems such as general atrophy will not occur. If, because of pain, the horse is compensating to avoid contact with the ground or weight bearing, or is not putting enough weight on the limb because of an imbalance in his action, swimming will help to balance the body development and even adjust unlevel action.

Adhesions, which can cause severe restrictions in the quality or extent of movement, have been successfully broken down by swimming. It can relax muscle spasms and nervous tension, and can aid in making the rest period more effective after exertion by increasing the circulation as described above. It can give a feeling of body well being, and a horse may feel as though he is on springs as the suspension comes back to the joints.

Horses often become very stressed when they are confined to the stable to reduce activity in an injured part. They cannot get rid of surplus energy so that when they recommence exercise they become excited and overexert their unfit muscles. The tissues that should be supporting the previously injured part are unable to do so and horses often reinjure themselves. Swimming is of great assistance in reducing the effects of confinement if regularly carried out during recuperation. It can be included in the fitness or rehabilitation programme of horses from many disciplines including racehorses, three-day eventers, dressage horses, polo ponies and police horses.

Swimming as part of a fitness programme

The horse swimming to maintain or improve cardiovascular fitness needs to achieve two things: first, to increase the supply of oxygen around the body and, secondly, to make the best use of the oxygen in the tissues. This requires a programme of work which stresses the systems involved so that they maintain or improve their efficiency; thus the heart rate, the cardiac output and arterial blood pressure are all involved.

The horse creates energy for muscle contraction and movement in two ways, aerobically and anaerobically. Aerobic respiration takes place at submaximal work loads when the heart rate is less than 200 beats per minute and glucose is 'burnt up' in the presence of oxygen to create energy. However, this process is limited by the speed at which the cardiovascular and respiratory systems can delivery oxygen to the muscles. At maximal work rates (HR over 200) oxygen just cannot be delivered quickly enough to supply the energy demands so that anaerobic respiration is used to 'top up' the energy supply. Energy is created from glucose in the absence of oxygen with the production of a poisonous by-product called lactic acid. Lactic acid is a major contributor to fatigue and its build-up in tissue should be avoided if a horse is to continue working. The horse's tolerance to lactic acid can be improved with training. It has been suggested that a 4-minute swim is equal to a 1-mile speed gallop. Research from different countries has produced differing values, perhaps due to the water being at a different temperature, etc. However, the authors' experience suggests that the equation is probably quite realistic.

Heart rates should be taken before, after and in some cases, during swimming, and the recovery times must be monitored and fitness levels recorded and compared just as in an interval training programme. Heart rate values are a good indicator of work effort and work load. The heart rate rises when constant effort turns to fatigue.

Once a horse is accustomed to swimming, heart rates of 141 to 171 beats per minute are regularly recorded which is equivalent to a 500 mpm canter in a reasonably fit horse. Thus swimming a horse for three 3-minute intervals is equivalent to cantering 1500 m three times (just under 1 mile) at a good ongoing speed. The effort needed to stay afloat is greater, and more work is required so the heart rate is as high for swimming as for cantering. The respiration rate during swimming, as with galloping, synchronises with the stride or rhythm of the action in the water so that it remains steady or rises only slightly during swimming. However, the respiratory rate will almost double after leaving the pool to help cool the horse and to repay the oxygen used up during exercise.

With natural swimming, the respiration rate should be 18 to 24 breaths per minute during swimming, increasing to 42 to 52 per minute afterwards. Restrictive or tethered swimming increases the work effort required as well as the work load, and must be carried out for short periods only.

Heart rates can be made to rise to 200 per minute by adopting a form of interval training in the pool, alternating natural swimming with restrictive swimming and rest and then repeating the process. This produces very good results as it exposes the horse to maximal work and helps the body systems to cope with anaerobic respiration. Swimming horses for too long a time can do more harm than good. Muscle development is also maintained and improved more efficiently by 'interval' swimming. If the horse is only allowed to swim for short intense periods at varying speeds with short rests for recovery, his muscles will develop for exercise rather than just keep him afloat.

If bad swimming techniques are used, muscle development will suffer. This can lead to people saying that using swimming in a fitness programme only teaches horses to win swimming races! Good techniques in swimming are just as important as they are in lungeing or riding, and knowledge and experience are necessary. Think what can happen to your carefully developed competition horse if he is lunged or ridden incorrectly, even just for a short time.

Teaching horses to swim correctly is a very important aspect of development. Bad techniques produce poor results and can give swimming a bad reputation. To start with, very short initial swims are recommended; allow the horse to enjoy it so that anxiety is banished along with any protective forms of behaviour. If the horse is swum in a tense attitude with his muscles tight, he will not use himself correctly; a little time spent in the beginning to ensure that he swims properly will reduce the risk of problems manifesting themselves later. This applies equally to a horse that has had a long break from swimming or one that swims badly because of unhappy experiences. Even if you think you are fit, think how unnerving a new type of activity can be. Cycling does not prepare you mentally for windsurfing!

Ideally, swimming and ground schooling will complement each other and form a good exercise programme if they can be combined. There are successful horses trained using swimming as their main form of exercise, but swimming alone is not normally a suitable, total, training programme. All training programmes must be tailored to each individual horse's needs and so must the therapy and the swimming elements that are included.

Artificial aids can be used to help support a horse or to alter his action in water. Some protection is necessary on the limbs; as with any exercise, horses can knock or overreach themselves and it is recommended that brushing boots be worn all round and overreach boots in front.

Swimming Pool Design

Swimming pools come in many different designs (Fig. 10.2). There are round ones, straight ones, and long oval shapes. Some pools combine the aspects of both straight and round design. Pools require a large capital outlay, and the design will depend to an extent upon how much you wish to spend and how frequently you will make use of it. Straight pools are less expensive, easier to manage and perhaps less dangerous. Round pools need to be large in circumference to eliminate the need for the horse to swim bent to one side. The swimming channel needs

Fig. 10.2 Swimming pool design.

to be only sufficiently wide to allow the horse to swim comfortably without striking the sides.

There are conflicting thoughts on the advantages and disadvantages of straight and round pools. It is held by some that if a horse swims straight his action will be more balanced and breathing will be easier if his body is not curved; in the round pool the horse's chest is compressed more on one side than on the other. Others believe that swimming in a circle will help the horse to achieve the suppleness necessary for dressage and jumping. A number of trainers of racehorses consider a straight pool to be too short a swim for their horses. However, for remedial work, a straight pool is perhaps the better design, and restricted swimming can be carried out more easily in a straight pool.

The British Blood Stock Agency have incorporated a straight swimming area with a traditional round pool; this is proving very satisfactory. While the horses are becoming accustomed to swimming they use the straight area, and when they are established swimmers they are introduced to swimming in a circle so that the length of the swim can be increased.

Hygiene in equine pools is of paramount importance, and this involves time and effort to maintain a high standard. There are the usual problems associated with human pools but in some cases the problems are greater; the water is treated with chemicals to kill bacteria and to keep the pH stable, and the prevention of growth of algae requires constant attention since such growth is more prevalent in pools exposed to sunlight. Large debris is dealt with by surface skimmers feeding to a filtration plant. Other chemicals can be used to help break down the debris into smaller particles which will disperse more readily.

Taking the cost of the pool, its housing, electricity for the pumps and the filtration plant, chemicals, and the manpower required to swim horses and to prepare and maintain the pool, it is obvious that swimming is expensive. These costs have to be matched against the benefits that swimming will give to a performance horse, especially if used as part of a routine.

Water Walks

Water walks provide very good remedial exercise. The horse is walked around in a depth of water which has a beneficial effect from the cushioning and the pulling. Walking itself is good exercise and often neglected; walking through water has the additional advantages of requiring further effort to move the limbs, with reduced concussion while still bearing weight. Good results can be obtained for strengthening the limbs.

Jacuzzis and Water Boots

Jacuzzis can be incorporated into a swimming pool for horses thus providing a water massage which is useful. The well known 'equine wellie boots' are a form of water massage or jacuzzi, and are used in many yards that have performance horses. The 'wellies' are shaped for horses' legs and are filled with water (hot, warm, cold or perhaps with some ice, herbs or salt). They have two therapeutic actions: that of the temperature of the water or solution, and the jacuzzi-like massage to the lower legs. The value of both actions has been explained. Provided the horse is not allowed to become chilled in the other parts of his body, water boots will aid the circulation of the lower limbs and control any inflammation from wear and tear.

11
Alternative Therapy

Herbs and Homeopathy

These treatments can be used to support the horse's health and its ability to cope with demanding activities.

Herbs

The feeding of herbs can be carried out by the owner or stable manager and will not add to demands on the precious commodity of time once incorporated into the routine. Indeed, in the long term, feeding herbs may save time and perhaps money. Feeding herbs can help prevent disease and other health problems occurring, although it must be remembered that not all diseases are preventable and much will depend upon the upbringing, age and genetics of each animal. The effects of feeding herbs are cumulative and act slowly. This is a considerable advantage, because it gives the body time to adjust and respond, preventing stressful imbalances from occurring. The benefits creep up on you! Common sense and moderation are important; feeding herbs to excess will not give better results and may well cause harm. The big advantage of including herbs in the horse's diet is that they can balance the body's systems, working on the whole horse: the circulatory, lymphatic, respiratory, digestive, nervous, muscular, skeletal, immune, reproductive, urinary and glandular systems will all benefit.

Any upset of homeostatic balance (the body's ability to maintain a stable internal balance of its various body processes) can cause health problems. The more we ask of the horse in terms of performance and travel, along with unnatural feeding habits and conditions, the more stress he is subjected to. In consequence his chances of full athletic function and resistance to bacterial and viral infections will increasingly depend upon the ability of the body to adjust the homeostatic balance.

This balance is jointly controlled by the nervous system, sending electrical messages, and by the glandular system, producing hormones — the chemical messages. These act together as a communications system throughout the body so that any subtle changes can be noted and appropriate remedial action can be taken.

The greater the demands on the horse the greater the pressure on these systems in terms of their nutrient requirement. There may be a need for nutrients that we have not yet identified. Herbs are consequently beneficial because they contain a vast number of nutrients and chemicals in a balanced form, especially when fed fresh in either solid or liquid form.

Herbs can be used as a medicine, in which case they are given in concentrated doses prescribed by a veterinary practitioner specialising in herbs. There appears to be an increase in this study, and you may find your own vet interested and informative. Many recognised medicines are produced from herbs. A specific part of the plant is extracted and used as an active agent. Herbalists suggest that this should not be done as the plant, seeds, root and bark are balanced entities and extracting just one or two active components will not produce the best results. The principle of feeding herbs is that the whole of the seed, the plant, the root or the bark is eaten, and the parts work together in complementarity. You can feed herbs as part of your horse's diet to act as a general support, or you can feed specific herbs to support a specific system.

Think of what we do to our horses' digestive systems: we give them additives, supplements and large quantities of concentrated foods, which are processed and highly fertilised, at times which are convenient to us. Add to this the medications, worming products, antibiotics, steroids and painkillers and you can see that their diet is vastly different from the one they would eat in their natural grazing habitat. All these ingredients may be necessary but they will inevitably have some side effects and possibly suppress some of the natural functions of the body.

Digestion is fundamental to all life processes. The saying 'You are what you eat' should really be 'You are what you absorb or assimilate'. If the horse cannot break down the food and absorb it properly, he will not reap the benefits of his carefully planned diet. Remember that the digestive system starts at the mouth and finishes in the large intestine and rectum. A more natural, high-fibre diet would be digested in the hind gut with the aid of microorganisms. This takes time and occupies a large volume. The highly concentrated diet of the performance horse is digested more quickly and earlier in the digestive system, in an unnatural process. The health and size of the microbial population in the hind gut will determine the efficiency of fibre digestion. These 'good' microbes can easily be destroyed by digestive disturbances, further upsetting the horse's digestive system.

Herbs supporting the digestive system are classified by their action. They include *demulcents*, which are rich in mucilage and which soothe and protect inflamed and irritated tissue; and *bitters*, which tone and normalise the digestive process and relieve absorption difficulties. The latter also help to stimulate the secretion of digestive enzymes and work on the glandular system, normalising any tendency towards over- or underactivity. *Anthelmintics* work against parasitic worms, and *carminatives* support the natural peristalsis (movement) of the intestines and the passage of materials through the system. *Antimicrobials* assist weak digestive systems which otherwise can become infected, or act as a support to the digestive system if the body is fighting infection in other areas. There are many other active ingredients in herbs that will support the horse's digestion. The skin and the coat of the horse will reflect his health; care and cleanliness will help to keep the coat and the skin healthy. Types of herbs that benefit the skin and coat include *vulneries*, which work by promoting the healing of minor cuts and wounds to the superficial tissues; *alteratives*, which alter and correct pollution of the blood and aid the condition of the skin and the coat; and antimicrobials, which help fight infection and cleanse the whole body. Herbs for the muscular and skeletal systems comprise the *antirheumatics*, the *anti-inflammatories*, the *rubefacients* (which are stimulatory), the *diuretics* (which cause increased excretion of urine), the *circulatory stimulants*, and *pain relievers*. Herbs for the circulatory system comprise the *heart tonics*, the *alteratives*, the *nervines* and the *antimicrobials*; this last group is especially important in the lymphatics. *Diuretics*, *urinary antiseptics*, *demulcents* and *astringents* benefit the kidneys, and *hormonal normalisers*, *uterine tonics*, *demulcents*, *nervines* and *antiseptics* act on the reproductive system. *Hepatics* are herbs that strengthen, tone and stimulate the secretory functions of the liver. The nervous system can benefit from the *nervine tonics*, *relaxants* and *stimulants*, which reduce stress, anxiety or overactivity. The respiratory system is very important to the equine athlete, not only in supplying oxygen, but also in acting as a means of excretion. By supporting the other organs of excretion we can take some of the load from the lungs which are constantly having to cope with infections, allergies, pollution and even lack of fresh air. The herbs used here include *expectorants*, *pectoral*, *demulcents*, *antispasmodics*, *antimicrobials* and *anticatarrhals*.

Table 11.1 lists herbs and their action and use.

Herbs can be grown easily, both to feed fresh and to preserve for winter use, and dried herbs may be purchased. It is important if dried herbs are to be used that they are properly harvested and stored. Herbs can be used for external problems and can act as healing agents and poultices. Some of these can be made up and kept for first-aid use.

Homeopathy

Homeopathic medicines can be used as a supportive in first aid and in veterinary treatments. The principle of homeopathic medication is that

Table 11.1 Herbs: action and use.

Symptom	Remedy
Abscess	Garlic, echinacea
Boil	Garlic, echinacea
Ulcer	Marigold, comfrey
Wart	Thuja, nettle
Eczema	Burdock
Itching	Marigold
Infection	Arnica
Cramps	Cramp bark, wild yam
Rheumatism	Cayenne, ginger
Pain	Cayenne, ginger
Sciatica	St John's wort

like cures like: the symptoms are matched to a medication that, in its original form would produce those symptoms. It has been described as having the ability to kick the body's natural defence system into action. In orthodox medicine, drugs are used to quell the symptoms of disease, not to stimulate them. The most well known homeopathic support to the equine athlete with all his stresses and strains is arnica. This is a derivative of a poisonous Swiss alpine plant and is used to treat bruises, strains and sprains.

The homeopathic medication is diluted so that the original substance is barely measurable. It is claimed that the energies of the substance are the curative elements. Homeopathic medicines come as small white pills, ointments and tinctures and are very safe and easy to administer. The pills and tinctures are best placed under the tongue so they dissolve near to the glands so that absorption is more direct.

Electrical Therapy: Laser, Ultrasound, Magnetic Fields, Muscle Stimulators, Vibrators

After an injury the owners of an equine athlete will ask the same questions that a human athlete will ask: how bad is it, and for how long will it reduce performance after recovery? These are understandable questions from a competitor's point of view when you consider the training, time and expense it has taken to achieve any performance level. Like humans, horses are individuals as are their injuries, and the degree of suffering varies accordingly. To the owner, speed of recovery is all important but this can be short sighted. As with the human athlete, the healing of an injury is only half of the problem; the other half is returning to full athletic potential. It is important that the best possible healing and full return to athletic potential are aimed for. This requires that a full recovery programme be followed, starting with immediate first aid.

Correct first aid can be one of the main factors in complete recovery and must be applied as soon as possible. Next comes a complete veterinary diagnosis, followed by prescribed medication and the recommended care. The vet will monitor the situation regularly, and he may recommend the use of a therapist skilled in the use of machines to help the tissue to heal in the best way and in the shortest time possible. He may let you use a machine yourself under his supervision. Once the tissue has healed, then comes rehabilitation, involving the use of machines, exercises and the start of refittening work.

This holistic approach (that the treatment involves the whole horse, not just his injuries) must also include stable management, nutrition and general care of the horse. You must look after his temperament, his confidence and his security. Your detailed assessment of his temperament made previously will show you how differently he is behaving and will thus indicate the degree of stress that he is under and the best way to manage his confinement and rehabilitation.

This, then, is the whole programme that will help the full recovery of the athlete after injury. If it is not carried out conscientiously, the chances of reinjury are high. This subsequent injury may affect the original site, or another part that suffered extra strain or compensation in the movement patterns.

There is no point in spending time, effort and money on the best veterinary treatments if the rehabilitation part of the programme is neglected. This has been proven over and over again with humans, and horse owners realising this have become fascinated by the use of therapy machines believing them to be miracle cures for all ills. This has led to indiscriminate use of potentially dangerous equipment and some strange reports on their use and the results achieved.

Many big yards have all the latest machines; some are in cupboards not being used, often because there is insufficient time to use them properly and the users have become disillusioned because the particular apparatus did not produce the results claimed. Other people do not like the idea of using them, believing that there has not been enough research into the effects on the horse, and some therapists find that they can do just as well by using their hands. Many think of rest as being the best form of treatment and others favour one machine for all problems, having no regard to its particular action on the tissues or other parts of the horse.

Good results can be achieved by the correct use of these machines. In some instances they do reduce the time of recovery, but their main advantage is in causing better healing. Remember: these machines are only tools, and although often very good tools their results will depend upon the capability of the person doing the work. A person who is trained and experienced in their use, who has a knowledge of the anatomy of the horse and its movement patterns, and who uses machines as part of a planned treatment and rehabilitation programme, will achieve better results. Obviously the best idea is to send the horse to a yard that specialises in this work and which has up to date knowledge of the use of these machines and the best facilities, where a whole programme can be planned and subsequently controlled and monitored.

If you decide to do the therapy yourself, ask your vet which mode of therapy he would recommend and then plan the programme as carefully as possible, perhaps with the help of this book, and monitor your results. Your vet may call in an expert for such methods as laser and ultrasound, but you should still know what can be done and how, and the contraindications if any, so that you can take appropriate action.

Laser

Laser stands for light amplification by stimulated emission of radiation. What happens is that the laser channels and organises the energy contained in white light. White light is diffused: it consists of a spectrum of colours each with a different wavelength. The laser concentrates the spectrum into a beam of high-energy infrared light. The word 'laser' suggests space-age weapons, but therapeutic lasers are low- to medium-power tools and the beam is designed to give a good safety factor. Two media that can be used for laser emission in physiotherapy are helium–neon (He–Ne) and gallium–arsenide (Ga–As). The Ga–As type gives an infrared emission of about 904 nanometres (a nanometre is one thousand millionth of a metre) and enables visible light to pass through the tissue layers without any critical rise in the temperature of the tissue. The infrared emission of radiation can act without discomfort to a depth of 35 mm. The helium–neon laser emits approximately 630 nanometres and only influences the superficial layers, and its emission of radiation are absorbed up to the first 4 mm.

Laser treatments can be pulsed or continuous, and there are differing views as to which gives the best results and which may in some cases inhibit healing. Treatments can be as short as a minute, but are usually longer depending on the treatment prescribed. Infrared lasers are able to penetrate tissue to a depth of up to 35 mm without producing significant heat in the superficial tissue. At this depth of penetration it is possible to produce a biological effect on the tissue without damage and with the acceleration of tissue repair.

The other important consideration is that of pain control; the relief of pain is very important because pain can decrease the healing time by not allowing the animal to rest in comfort. The laser can ease pain and may be better than administering drugs with their possible side effects. Lasers may only take the pain away temporarily without healing, which can cause problems: the owner thinks that the horse has recovered enough to increase his work, or, having been confined for a period and having had his pain reduced, the horse resents his confinement and starts doing silly things in his box. The reduction of pain by use of the laser coupled with controlled rehabilitation exercises and careful monitoring will help to ensure that the pain relief is permanent and that healing continues.

When laser is applied to a horse, the beam must strike at an angle of 90° otherwise it will reduce the effect. The laser is usually applied every other day, at the site of injury or at the acupuncture or trigger points. One to ten sessions may be necessary. Where practicable, the coat should be clipped and the area cleaned so that it is free of any light-sensitive drugs such as iodine or furacin. Different treatments will require different power densities. Power density is the number of watts (W); the power in watts or frequency/plus repetition rate is measured in hertz (Hz) and the pulse width/pulse repetition rate is measured in nanometres (nm).

Although laser machines are made to be very safe, certain precautions are necessary. The animal should be on a rubber surface and the operator should wear goggles. Lasers should not be used on pregnant mares or on animals with heart problems.

Ultrasound

Ultrasound or ultrasonic waves are sound waves with a pitch above the upper limits of human hearing. The uses of ultrasound are many and varied, and include submarine echoes, flaw detection, the monitoring of tissue density and changes, and therapeutic treatment to influence the healing of tissue.

Ultrasonic waves are normally produced by causing a solid object to vibrate with a high frequency; therapeutic frequencies are in the range of 1 to 3 MHz and machines are usually 1 MHz or 1 to 3 MHz. For a machine of 1 MHz a vibrating source with a frequency of one million cycles per second is needed. In therapeutic ultrasound machines, these vibrations are usually achieved by the use of a quartz crystal to produce the correct frequency. The crystal is fused to the metal plate of the treatment or transducer head to produce the ultrasonic wave. This head is sealed for safety reasons.

Ultrasonic waves obey the laws of refraction (the change of direction which rays undergo when passing from one medium to another) and reflection (the angle caused by reflected rays). Thus the treatment head should be perpendicular to the part being treated to give the full effect. If this is not possible, the part should be immersed in boiled water which has cooled, this prevents refraction of the waves which would result in the area you intend to treat being missed.

Air will not transmit ultrasonic waves and they are reflected instead of being transmitted. If reflection occurs, the ultrasonic beam will reflect back to the treatment head which can damage the crystal. With this in mind the ultrasonic beam should not be turned on until the treatment head is well covered in a coupling medium which transmits the waves to the area to be treated. Where body structure changes cause reflection of ultrasound, for example between the periosteum and the bone, a concentrated heating effect can be created. When reflection from bone occurs, there is twice the intensity of ultrasound in the area, which can cause damage without the horse warning you as the pain-sensitive nerves are not affected.

A coupling medium is used between the treatment head and the area that is being treated. No coupling medium gives perfect transmission to the patient, and only the recommended coupling should be used.

To test to see if the machine is working, apply a generous amount of coupling medium to the treatment head and turn the intensity up. The coupling will bubble when the machine is operational. This can also be done under water.

The deeper the ultrasound waves penetrate, the more absorption and scattering reduce the intensity. The term 'half value distance' means that the intensity at the deep tissue levels is only half the intensity at the surface. You cannot increase the surface power in the hope that you are reaching the deeper tissue as the superficial tissue will suffer.

In some machines there is a fixed pulse mode and in others the pulse can be varied. Some machines are rated M.S., 'M' denoting the time the wave is active and 'S' denoting inactivity. In general terms the pulsed mode is considered to be less heating. The thermal effect of continuous ultrasound is absorbed by the tissue and converted to heat if the treatment head is held in a stationary position. Excessive heat can result in tissue burns. These points should all be in the instructions which should be read carefully before using the machine.

Ultrasound stimulates blood flow and cell activity and hence healing, but it should not be used in cases of acute sepsis because of the danger of spreading infection, nor in tumor treatment, on pregnant animals or on those with heart problems.

Treatment times depend on many factors and whether the injury is acute or chronic. In the acute stage of an injury, caution must be exercised and the dosage kept low: 0.25 or 0.5 W cm^{-2} is recommended for 3 to 4 minutes using a pulsed beam to prevent heating. The pulse ratio may be varied, but normally 1:7 should be used in acute cases and 1:1 when less acute.

With chronic cases, start low at first $(0.8\,\mathrm{W\,cm^{-2}})$, in the pulsed mode, then change to continuous mode for approximately 4 minutes. The 3 MHz machine is normally used for superficial lesions and the 1 MHz for deeper tissues. Treatment times, modes and intensities are difficult to specify as there are so many variables. This is where experienced operators who have treated many different problems will be able to judge the best course of treatment. They will also be guided by the condition of the injury before and after treatment.

Magnetic Field Therapy

There is a choice of machines and equipment which provide static or pulsed magnetic field therapy. These range from large machines using mains electricity to smaller machines utilising a battery or simple magnetic foil. All equipment is different and you should follow the manufacturer's instructions and suggested treatment guides carefully.

The magnetic foil can be incorporated into a pair of boots or fitted to any part of the body requiring treatment. The larger machines use a pulsing electromagnetic field which is set up around the area to be treated by adaptors which can be positioned by the use of velcro on a cotton sheet. The time, frequency and intensity of the field are all variable, and these are known to be very important factors in treatment, but more research is needed in this area to analyse how they interrelate.

The therapeutic value which is claimed for pulsed magnetic fields is that by increasing the metabolic rate of cells they accelerate the healing process. Although results are difficult to evaluate, in practice it has been found that magnetic fields increase the circulation in superficial tissue, which inevitably has some effect on the deeper tissue. Magnetic field therapy would also appear to benefit chronic problems; magnets have been applied to stimulate acupuncture points for hundreds of years.

Some scientists believe that the earth's magnetic field is reducing, and that this may be causing health problems from magnetic deficiency, especially for people and animals who spend a lot of time in insulated buildings and cars. There is also a theory that overexposure to artificial pulsating magnetic fields can be detrimental to health. In some countries sites are tested for this before building is allowed.

Electrical Stimulation of Muscles

This works on the principle that an electric current can stimulate a motor point and so produce a contraction of the muscle, allowing increased circulation, this is helpful where muscles have atrophied, are weak or become imbalanced, and the movement patterns have compensated. Muscles work in groups to cause, prevent and support the movement of joints, and there is a fine balance between each of these groups. Over, under or imbalanced development within these groups will affect the stability of the joint.

Some muscle stimulating machines can be used to contract muscle only; others can be used on different tissues to increase cell activity and restore ionic balance in damaged tissue.

Transcutaneous Electrical Nerve Stimulators

These machines (TENS) produce low voltage electrical pulses to the nervous system. An electrical current is passed through the skin via electrodes to the nerve receptors, helping to relieve pain.

Electrical Vibrators

These machines vibrate the tissue and help circulation. They can be used before and after strenuous or stressful activity, particularly in areas which will benefit from an increased blood supply.

12
Developing the rider's athletic potential

Passenger or part of a team? Are you helping your horse to be an athletic performer or making it more difficult for him? Do you disturb his balance? Are you one-sided? Have you a stiff back? If you have a stiff back, no doubt your horse has.

Bad Riding Technique

For the horse's sake always get the best instructor you can afford. Make sure you feel the instruction is right for you, your body, your horse and your philosophy. Once you have decided this, place your confidence in that instructor, he or she will get to know you and your horse well. One of the worst things is to have too many instructors telling you different things. This can cause confusion: they may all be right, but communication can be misinterpreted causing problems.

As humans we are all different in biomechanical detail and development. Although our bodies, with different development and training, will accommodate to a position in the saddle which allows good contact and feel with the horse, economy of control and good balance, a lot will depend on the individual shape (biomechanics). If you are forced into an unnatural position, discomfort will make you compensate and your balance will become unstable and unequal and will affect the horse.

Posture

Good posture in horses and their riders is essential for good athletic function. Good posture for the rider simply means a posture in which the body can function economically and effectively without unnecessary fatigue, stiffness, discomfort and pain. The rider may have old injuries which have healed tightly, or is compensating which affects his functional movement patterns; these will prevent good posture.

If possible, have your back and body assessed for your sport by a sports therapist and have treatment where necessary to restore maximum suppleness and strength, equal development and balance. Do not forget: a lot of back problems are compensatory ones from other areas. You will be given advice on your everyday posture. The Alexander technique will help to maintain correct posture after treatment.

To protect your back and prevent injury it is essential to perfect the posture known as the pelvic tilt. If your pelvis is balanced, your back is protected and your back muscle less vulnerable to injury. The pelvic tilt must be learnt. Lie on your back on the floor *with knees bent*. Place your hands between the floor and the hollow of your back. Flatten your lower back against your hands by using the stomach muscles to tilt the pelvis up and back. Further tighten your stomach muscles and hold this position for a count of 5 while breathing slowly and deeply. Many people hold their breath when using their abdominal muscles. Relax the stomach muscles and feel the pelvis roll out of the balanced position. If you do this as an exercise to increase your abdominal muscle tone and control, start by doing this four times and increase as you become fitter. This will make sure you are using the correct muscles.

Being in Balance

We have mentioned balance, imbalance and balance development. What do these terms mean? Being in balance with your horse is perhaps the most important factor in riding. This balance should eliminate the need to grip or hang on to the horse; the gripping will stiffen the horse's back. The rider's balance is adjusted to the horse's centre of gravity and the rider moves with the horse. Balanced development is the symmetrical development of the rider's body, which is difficult to achieve but none the less important. Effort must be applied to do work equally with the left side and the right side of the body and increase the exercises for the weaker side. Functional imbalance of the rider can affect the horse's way of going, and conversely imbalances in the horse can affect the rider. No rider or horse is perfect, but to ride well and to make sure our horses are not limited in their performance it means we must work hard to achieve a balanced body.

The rider can be the cause of a lot of horse performance problems, preventing horses from producing their full potential. We have been told this many times but how can we, or our riding, help to ensure that our horse's development is correct? The answers include hard work and attention to detail.

One of the main factors to consider is whether or not you are physically fit enough to ride. For the horse's sake you should not ride to get fit: you should be fit to ride. This is where bad posture, poor technique, fatigue and compensations in the rider's balance may cause problems in the horse.

You can test your level of fitness to ride and evaluate your strength and suppleness, especially of your back, by completing the following tests and monitoring the results. This is particularly valuable after a lay-off from riding. If you have any medical problems, consult your doctor before carrying out these tests.

Self-assessment for Fitness

Evaluation of General Fitness

To evaluate your general fitness levels, take your pulse at rest. The pulse in the neck or wrist is easy to locate with the fingertips, but do not press too hard on the artery. Record your finding over 1 minute.

Using a pile of large books, a box or a step about 20 cm (8 in) high, step up and down briskly for 3 minutes. If at any time you feel uncomfortable, stop. Rest for 1 minute and take your pulse. The lower the pulse rate increase the fitter you are.

	Pulse rate increase	
	Men	Women
Excellent	Below 68	Below 76
Good	68–79	76–85
Average	80–89	86–94
Below average	90–99	90–109
Very poor	100+	110+

If your score is average or better, you should be fit enough to start gaining fitness for your competition riding. If below average or worse, you should undertake a fitness programme. Record your score and date this self-assessment so you can monitor it regularly. You can check your strength and suppleness, especially of your back, by doing the tests described here and recording the results in Table 12.1.

The Back Fitness Tests

It is a good idea to keep these monitoring assessments with your horse's profile and check them regularly, especially if you do other sports or activities which tend to develop one side or part of the body more than others.

Test A — The sit-up

The major purpose of Test A (Fig. 12.1) is to determine the flexibility of the back. Its minor purpose is to determine the strength of the stomach muscles.

Table 12.1 Monitor your fitness levels (*Not exercises but tests*).

	Date	No.	Score	Date	No.	Score	Date etc . . . .
1. *Sit-ups* To test flexibility of your back							
2. *Legs* To determine the strength of abdominal muscle							
3. *Lateral trunk* $\frac{1}{2}$ marks R $\frac{1}{2}$ marks L To determine strength of the lateral muscles of trunk and legs							
4. *Hip flexors* R L To determine strength of hip flexors							

Score: 4–5 = very good, 6–9 = average, 10–13 = fair, 14–16 = poor. If you are over 45, subtract 2 from each of your totals. Check your fitness level after illness, injury or any lay-off from riding; it will help you and help your horse. Your fatigue can injure your horse. Do not cause yourself pain while doing tests. If painful, stop and get the problem checked.

Score	Performance	Back fitness
1	Able to sit up with knees bent and hands behind the neck.	Excellent: adequate spinal flexibility and stomach strength.
2	Able to sit up with knees bent and arms folded across the chest.	Good: need to improve stomach muscle strength.
3	Able to sit up with knees bent and arms held out straight.	Fair: need to improve spinal flexibility and stomach strength.
4	Unable to sit up with the knees bent.	Poor: need a great deal of improvement in both strength and flexibility.

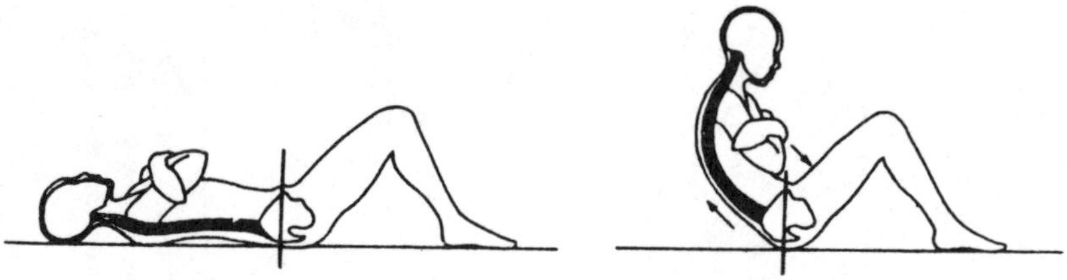

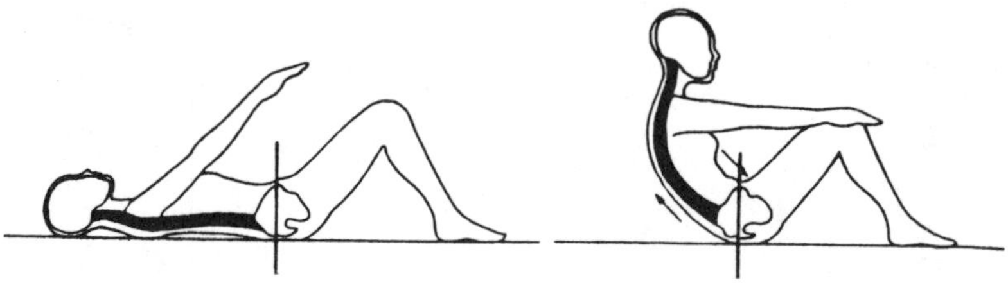

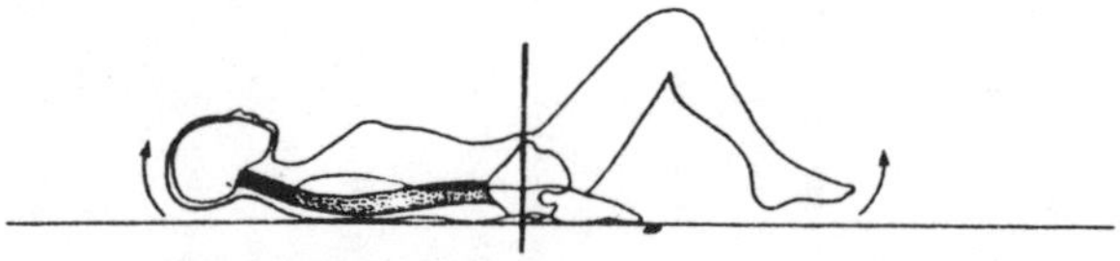

Fig. 12.1 The sit-up.

(1) Lie on your back on the floor.
(2) Bend your knees to a 45° angle, placing your feet flat on the floor.
(3) Place your hands behind your neck.
(4) Slowly and smoothly try to sit up without raising your feet off the floor. If you are unable to sit up without your feet coming off the floor:
(5) Place your arms across your chest and try to sit up again. If still unable to sit up:
(6) Put your arms out straight and try once more to sit up.

Do not jerk yourself up or crank your head up with your arms. This can aggravate a neck problem. For a valid test the effort must be made slowly and smoothly. *Do not* tuck your feet under something or have someone hold them down. This invalidates the test. It makes it easier to perform because it activates the leg muscles, which pull the back to a sitting position. Pulling yourself up in this way can also harm a weak back.

Figure 12.1 shows the four performance levels for Test A and the scores assigned to each.

Many people are distressed when they fail such a simple test. This is particularly true of athletic types who appear quite muscular. What they have forgotten is that flexibility or suppleness of the back is just as important for fitness as strong stomach muscles. People who do quite poorly on Test A often include:

- Older people whose backs have naturally stiffened.
- Muscular individuals who have not maintained suppleness and flexibility. They often feel that they fail Test A because their upper body weight causes their feet to lift up off the ground. However, individuals with good flexibility have an ability to change their centre of gravity, allowing them to sit up despite upper body bulk.
- Individuals who have suffered back problems that have left their backs stiff.
- Individuals with pot bellies, indicating poor abdominal muscle tone and strength.
- In general, women perform this test at a higher level than men because they have better flexibility.

Test B — Double straight leg raise

Test B determines the strength of the abdominal or stomach muscles.

(1) Lie on your back on the floor with your legs straight out in front of you.

(2) Place your hands between the hollow of your back and the floor.

(3) Eliminate the hollow between your back and the floor by tightening your stomach muscles and forcing your back tightly against your hands on the floor. There should be no space. *Keep your back held tightly against the floor*. This is very important.

(4) Firmly hold this position and simultaneously raise both feet ten inches off the floor.

(5) Hold the feet up for ten counts keeping the back tightly pressed against the floor.

Caution: If your lower back begins to curve after raising your legs or if back pain is felt, do not continue. Back strain may result from lifting the legs when the back is not held in the flat, balanced, pelvic position. Remember that this is a test and not an exercise. Once you have determined your score, stop the testing. This test can be harmful if it is performed continuously while the back is weak.

Figure 12.2 shows the four performance levels for Test B and the scores assigned to each.

Curling the head off the floor makes the test easier. Your body, including your head, should be held *straight out* to make the test valid. Lifting the legs too high also makes the test easier and invalidates it. It is most important to *keep the hollow of the back flat against the floor* because this determines the grade. Most people tend to concentrate, instead, on the effort of raising the legs.

Everyone should aim for grade 1 on this test. Age is no barrier to good performance provided the stomach muscles are strong enough. This test shows whether the stomach muscles can hold the balanced pelvic position under stressful conditions, such as when you are playing sports or lifting heavy objects. It also shows whether you have the ability to flatten the back and eliminate the hollow in the lower back when your legs are held straight out. If you can't eliminate the hollow, bend your knees and try again. If you can get rid of the hollow when your knees are bent, it indicates that you have short hip flexors and you will do poorly on Test D.

Test C — Lateral trunk lift

Test C determines the strength of the lateral muscles of the trunk and legs.

(1) You will need someone to assist you in this test. Lie on your right side with your legs straight out and look straight ahead.

(2) Fold your arms across your chest.

Score	Performance	Back fitness
1	Able to keep the back flat while raising the legs for ten seconds.	Excellent: can demonstrate balanced pelvic position and hold it under extreme stress.
2	Able to raise the legs for several seconds, but the back curves part way through the test.	Good: can demonstrate balanced pelvic position, but need more stomach muscle strength and training to hold good posture under extreme stress.
3	Able to lift the legs, but the back curves as soon as the legs are raised.	Fair: need training in balanced pelvic position and increased stomach muscle strength.
4	Unable to lift both legs.	Poor: need extensive training in balanced pelvic position and increased stomach muscle strength.

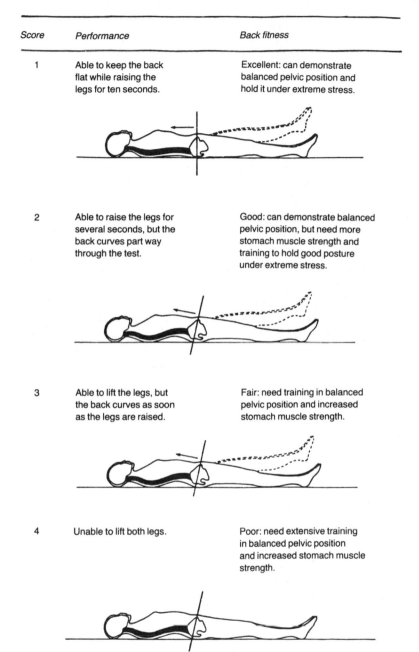

Fig. 12.2 Double straight leg raise.

(3)   Have your assistant firmly hold your feet down by the ankles so that they do not rise off the floor during the test.

(4)   Slowly and smoothly raise your shoulders and upper body off the floor.

(5)   Raise your shoulders up as far as possible and hold for ten counts.

(6)   Return to the starting position.

(7)   Repeat, testing the other side of your body.

Caution: If there is pain or discomfort, stop the test.

Figure 12.3 shows the four performance levels for Test C and the scores assigned to each.

Do not jerk or jump the body up; this invalidates the test. So does pushing up from the elbow. Your body must be perfectly straight while lying on your side. Many people substitute other muscle groups by allowing the body to drift forwards or backwards while they are lifting the upper body.

This test determines the strength of the lateral trunk and leg muscles, which are critical for upright posture. When you are lying on your right side, you are testing the muscles in your left side and vice versa. People who experience fatigue or discomfort in the lower back after jogging, long walks, or forward bending (while sweeping or raking, for example), usually do poorly on this test. It is important to compare the performance on the right and left sides. A poor performance on just one side of the body usually correlates with past injury to the side being tested.

Test D — Knee flexion

This determines the length of the hip flexors.

(1)   Lie on your back on the floor with your legs straight out in front of you.

(2)   Eliminate the hollow between your back and the floor as before (see Test B).

(3)   Raise and bend on knee, clasping it with both hands, and bring the knee to your chest keeping the other leg flat on the floor.

Figure 12.4 shows the four performance levels for Test D.

The Instructor's Role

If you are a riding instructor, the more you can communicate precisely which part of the body, bones and muscle you are talking about the better. Start by defining your meanings to make sure your rider inter-

Score	Performance	Back fitness
1	Able to raise the upper body completely and hold for ten counts.	Excellent: adequate lateral trunk muscles.

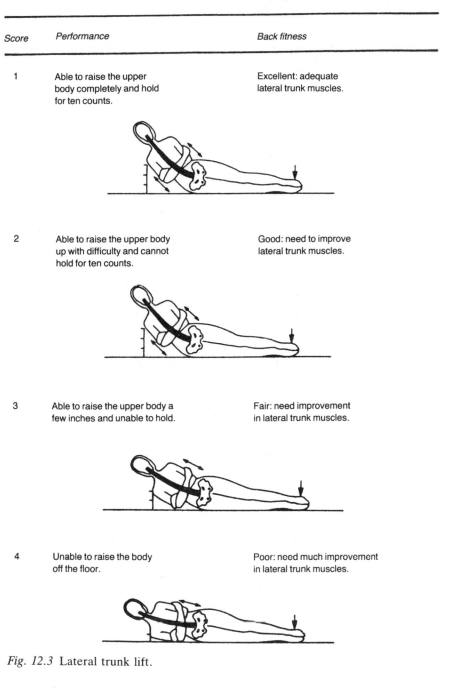

2	Able to raise the upper body up with difficulty and cannot hold for ten counts.	Good: need to improve lateral trunk muscles.
3	Able to raise the upper body a few inches and unable to hold.	Fair: need improvement in lateral trunk muscles.
4	Unable to raise the body off the floor.	Poor: need much improvement in lateral trunk muscles.

Fig. 12.3 Lateral trunk lift.

Score	Performance	Back fitness
1	Able to bring your knee completely to chest and keep the other leg flat on the floor.	Excellent: hip flexors are the proper length.
2	Able to bring your knee to your chest but the other leg lifts slightly off the floor.	Good: need to slightly stretch hip flexors.
3	Leg lifts completely off the floor when your knee is pulled to your chest.	Fair: need much improvement in hip flexors length.
4	Leg flies up into the air when your knee is held against your chest.	Poor: inadequate length of hip flexors — they need a great deal of stretching.

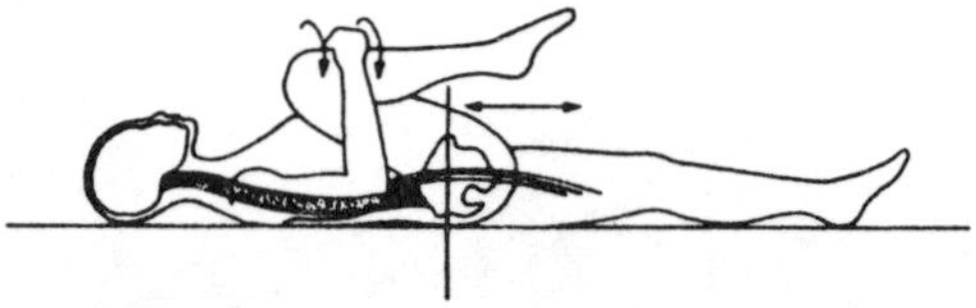

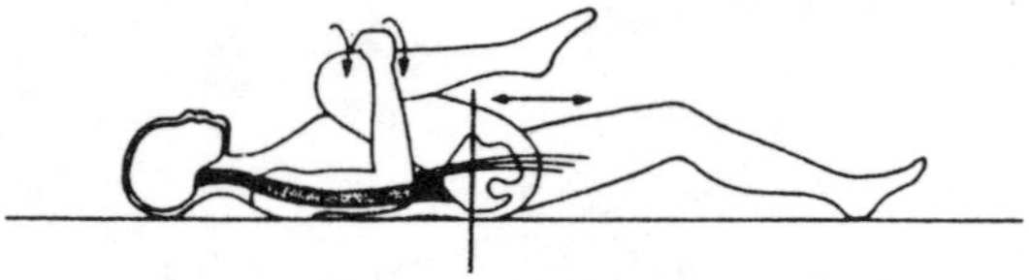

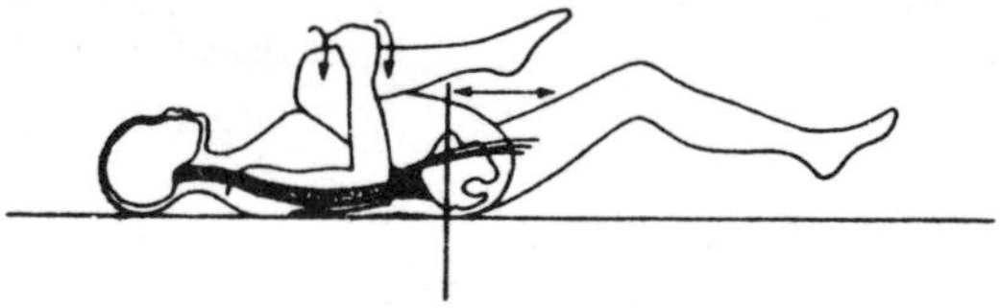

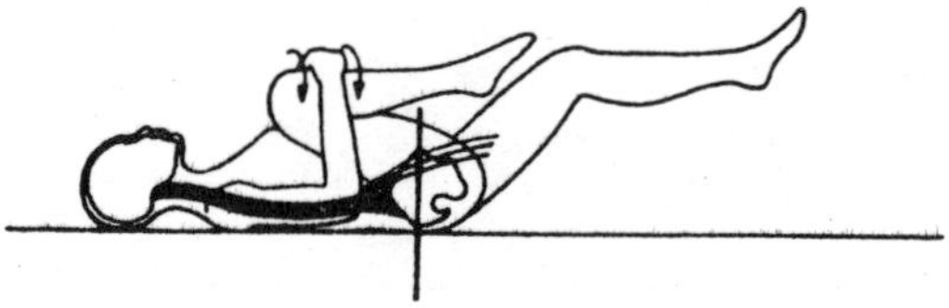

Fig. 12.4 Knee flexion.

prets your intention correctly. It is important to know the difference in anatomy between men and women; the structure of the lower back, sacrum, pelvis and thighs is different. Both sexes will have physical difficulties of different types when perfecting the art of riding. The pelvic and hip articulation are quite different in men and women. The part of the pelvis you sit on — the seat bones or ischia — are quite different and give different problems to overcome. It should be part of an instructor's education to study the difference in the anatomy of both sexes and to look at the different biomechanics of the human body and the problems they may give to the rider.

Index